$8.00
n

Heritage BUILDERS

P9-AOQ-559

Family Night

Tool Chest

Wisdom Life Skills

Creating Lasting Impressions for the Next Generation

Jim Weidmann and Kurt Bruner
with Mike and Amy Nappa

Chariot VICTOR
PUBLISHING
A DIVISION OF COOK COMMUNICATIONS

This book is dedicated to Rick Osborne and the "Lightwave" team.
Thanks for the encouragement and help as we began.

ChariotVictor Publishing
a division of Cook Communications, Colorado Springs, Colorado 80918
Cook Communications, Paris, Ontario
Kingsway Communications, Eastbourne, England.

HERITAGE BUILDERS/FAMILY NIGHT TOOL CHEST—WISDOM LIFE SKILLS
© 1998 by Jim Weidmann and Kurt Bruner

First edition 1998

Edited by Eric Stanford
Design by Bill Gray
Cover and Interior Illustrations by Guy Wolek

ISBN 0-7814-3015-1

Printed and bound in the United States of America
02 01 00 99 98   5 4 3 2 1

Heritage Builders/Family Night Tool Chest—Wisdom Life Skills is a Heritage Builders book, created in association with the authors at Nappaland Communications. To contact Heritage Builders Association, send e-mail to: Hbuilders@aol.com.

Contents

The Heritage Builders Series

This resource was created as an outreach of the Heritage Builders Association—a network of families and churches committed to passing a strong heritage to the next generation. Designed to motivate and assist families as they become intentional about the heritage passing process, this series draws upon the collective wisdom of parents, grandparents, church leaders, and family life experts, in an effort to provide balanced, biblical parenting advice along with effective, practical tools for family living. For more information on the goals and work of the Heritage Builders Association, please see page 117.

Kurt Bruner, M.A.
Executive Editor
Heritage Builders Series

⊚ Introduction

There is toothpaste all over the plastic-covered table. Four young kids are having the time of their lives squeezing the paste out of the tube—trying to expunge every drop like Dad told them to. "Okay," says Dad, slapping a twenty-dollar bill onto the table. "The first person to get the toothpaste back into their tube gets this money!" Little hands begin working to shove the peppermint pile back into rolled-up tubes—with very limited success.

Jim is in the midst of a weekly routine in the Weidmann home when he and his wife spend time creating "impression points" with the kids. "We can't do it, Dad!" protests the youngest child.

"The Bible tells us that's just like your tongue. Once the words come out, it's impossible to get them back in. You need to be careful what you say because you may wish you could take it back." An unforgettable impression is made.

Impression points occur every day of our lives. Intentionally or not, we impress upon our children our values, preferences, beliefs, quirks, and concerns. It happens both through our talk and through our walk. When we do it right, we can turn them on to the things we believe. But when we do it wrong, we can turn them off to the values we most hope they will embrace. The goal is to find ways of making this reality work for us, rather than against us. How? By creating and capturing opportunities to impress upon the next generation our values and beliefs. In other words, through what we've labeled impression points.

The kids are all standing at the foot of the stairs. Jim is at the top of that same staircase. They wait eagerly for Dad's instructions.

"I'll take you to Baskin Robbins for ice cream if you can figure how to get up here." He has the attention of all four kids. "But there are a few rules. First, you can't touch the stairs. Second, you can't touch the railing. Now, begin!"

After several contemplative moments, the youngest speaks up. "That's impossible, Dad! How can we get to where you are without touching the stairs or the railing?"

After some disgruntled agreement from two of the other children, Jacob gets an idea. "Hey, Dad. Come down here." Jim walks down the stairs. "Now bend over while I get on your back. Okay, climb the stairs."

Bingo! Jim proceeds to parallel this simple game with how it is impossible to get to God on our own. But when we trust Christ's completed work on our behalf, we can get to heaven. A lasting impression is made. After a trip up the stairs on Dad's back, the whole gang piles into the minivan for a double scoop of mint-chip.

Six years ago, Jim and his wife Janet began setting aside time to intentionally impress upon the kids their values and beliefs through a weekly ritual called "family night." They play games, talk, study, and do the things which reinforce the importance of family and faith. It is during these times that they intentionally create these impression points with their kids. The impact? The kids are having fun and a heritage is being passed.

intentional or "oops"?

Sometimes, we accidentally impress the wrong things on our kids rather than intentionally impressing the right things. But there is an effective, easy way to change that. Routine family nights are a powerful tool for creating intentional impression points with our children.

The concept behind family nights is rooted in a biblical mandate summarized in Deuteronomy 6:5-9.

> *"Love the LORD your God with all your heart and with all your soul and with all your strength. These commandments that I give you today are to be upon your hearts. Impress them on your children."*
> ***How?***
> *"Talk about them when you sit at home and when you walk along the road, when you lie down and when you get up. Tie them as symbols on your hands and bind them on your foreheads. Write them on the doorframes of your houses and on your gates."*

In other words, we need to take advantage of every opportunity to impress our beliefs and values in the lives of our children. A growing network of parents are discovering family nights to be a highly effective, user-friendly approach to doing just that. As one father put it ,"This has changed our entire family life." And another dad, "Our investment of time and energy into family nights has more eternal value than we may ever know." Why? Because they are intentionally teaching their children at the wisdom level, the level at which the children understand and can apply eternal truths.

☺ truth is a treasure

Two boys are running all over the house, carefully following the complex and challenging instructions spelled out on the "truth treasure map" they received moments ago. An earlier map contained a few rather simple instructions that were much easier to follow. But the "false treasure box" it lead to left something to be desired. It was empty. Boo Dad! They hope for a better result with map number two.

STEP ONE:

Walk sixteen paces into the front family room.

STEP TWO:

Spin around seven times, then walk down the stairs.

STEP THREE:

Run backwards to the other side of the room.

STEP FOUR:

Try and get around Dad and climb under the table.

You get the picture. The boys are laughing at themselves, complaining to Dad, and having a ball. After twenty minutes of treasure hunting they finally reach the elusive "truth treasure box." Little hands open the lid, hoping for a better result this time around. They aren't disappointed. The box contains a nice selection of their favorite candies. Yea Dad!

"Which map was easier to follow?" Dad asks.

"The first one," comes their response.

"Which one was better?"

"The second one. It led to a true treasure," says the oldest.

"That's just like life," Dad shares, "Sometimes it's easier to follow what is false. But it is always better to seek and follow what is true."

They read from Proverbs 2 about the hidden treasure of God's truth and end their time repeating tonight's jingle—"It's best for you to seek what's true." Then they indulge themselves with a mouthful of delicious candy!

☉ the power of family nights

The power of family nights is twofold. First, it creates a formal setting within which Dad and Mom can intentionally instill beliefs, values, or character qualities within their child. Rather than defer to the influence of peers and media, or abdicate character training to the school and church, parents create the opportunity to teach their children the things that matter most.

The second impact of family nights is perhaps even more significant than the first. Twenty to sixty minutes of formal fun and instruction can set up countless opportunities for informal reinforcement. These informal impression points do not have to be created, they just happen—at the dinner table, while driving in the car, while watching television, or any other parent/child time together. Once you have formally discussed a given family night topic, you and your children will naturally refer back to those principles during the routine dialogues of everyday life.

If the truth were known, many of us hated family devotions while growing up. We had them sporadically at best, usually whenever our parents were feeling particularly guilty. But that was fine, since the only thing worse was a trip to the dentist. Honestly, do we really think that is what God had in mind when He instructed us to teach our children? As an alternative, many parents are discovering family nights to be a wonderful complement to or replacement for family devotions as a means of passing their beliefs and values to the kids. In fact, many parents hear their kids ask at least three times per week:

"Can we have family night tonight?"

Music to Dad's and Mom's ears!

@ Keys to Effective Family Nights

There are several keys which should be incorporated into effective family nights.

MAKE IT FUN!

Enjoy yourself, and let the kids have a ball. They may not remember everything you say, but they will always cherish the times of laughter—and so will you.

KEEP IT SIMPLE!

The minute you become sophisticated or complicated, you've missed the whole point. Don't try to create deeply profound lessons. Just try to reinforce your values and beliefs in a simple, easy-to-understand manner. Read short passages, not long, drawn-out sections of Scripture. Remember: The goal is to keep it simple.

DON'T DOMINATE!

You want to pull them into the discovery process as much as possible. If you do all the talking, you've missed the mark. Ask questions, give assignments, invite participation in every way possible. They will learn more when you involve all of their senses and emotions.

GO WITH THE FLOW!

It's fine to start with a well-defined outline, but don't kill spontaneity by becoming overly structured. If an incident or question leads you in a different direction, great! Some of the best impression opportunities are completely unplanned and unexpected.

MIX IT UP!

Don't allow yourself to get into a rut or routine. Keep the sense of excitement and anticipation through variety. Experiment to discover what works best for your family. Use books, games, videos, props, made-up stories, songs, music or music videos, or even go on a family outing.

DO IT OFTEN!

We tend to find time for the things that are really important. It is best to set aside one evening per week (the same evening if possible) for family night. Remember, repetition is the best teacher. The more impressions you can create, the more of an impact you will make.

MAKE A MEMORY!

Find ways to make the lesson stick. For example, just as advertisers create"jingles" to help us remember their products, it is helpful to create family night "jingles" to remember the main theme—such as "It's best for you to seek what's true" or "Just like air, God is there!"

USE OTHER TOOLS FROM THE HERITAGE BUILDERS TOOL CHEST!

Family night is only one exciting way for you to intentionally build a loving heritage for your family. You'll also want to use these other exciting tools from Heritage Builders.

The Family Fragrance: There are five key qualities to a healthy family fragrance, each contributing to an environment of love in the home. It's easy to remember the Fragrance Five by fitting them into an acrostic using the word "Aroma"—

A—Affection
R—Respect
O—Order
M—Merriment
A—Affirmation

Impression Points: Ways that we impress on our children our values, preferences, and concerns. We do it through our talk and our actions. We do it intentionally (through such methods as Family Nights), and we do it incidentally.

The Right Angle: The Right Angle is the standard of normal healthy living against which our children will be able to measure their atttitudes, actions, and beliefs.

Traditions: Meaningful activities which the process of passing on emotional, spiritual, and relational inheritance between generations. Family traditions can play a vital role in this process.

Please see the back of the book for information on how to receive the FREE Heritage Builders Newsletter which contains more information about these exciting tools! Also, look for the new book, *The Heritage*, available at your local Christian bookstore.

@ How to Use This Tool Chest

Summary page: For those who like the bottom line, we have provided a summary sheet at the start of each family night session. This abbreviated version of the topic briefly highlights the goal, key Scriptures, activity overview, main points, and life slogan. On the reverse side of this detachable page there is space provided for you to write down any ideas you wish to add or alter as you make the lesson your own.

Step-by-step: For those seeking suggestions and directions for each step in the family night process, we have provided a section which walks you through every activity, question, Scripture reading, and discussion point. Feel free to follow each step as written as you conduct the session, or read through this portion in preparation for your time together.

À la carte: We strongly encourage you to use the material in this book in an "à la carte" manner. In other words, pick and choose the questions, activities, Scriptures, age-appropriate ideas, etc. which best fit your family. This book is not intended to serve as a curriculum, requiring compliance with our sequence and plan, but rather as a tool chest from which you can grab what works for you and which can be altered to fit your family situation.

The long and the short of it: Each family night topic presented in this book includes several activities, related Scriptures, and possible discussion items. Do not feel it is necessary to conduct them all in a single family night. You may wish to spread one topic over several weeks using smaller portions of each chapter, depending upon the attention span of the kids and the energy level of the parents. Remember, short and effective is better than long and thorough.

Journaling: Finally, we have provided space with each session for you to capture a record of meaningful comments, funny happenings, and unplanned moments which will inevitably occur during family night. Keep a notebook of these journal entries for future reference. You will treasure this permanent record of the heritage passing process for years to come.

1: Pop Quiz

Exploring why God allows trials and tests

Scripture
- James 1:2-4—Trials help us grow.
- James 1:12—God rewards us after He tests us.

ACTIVITY OVERVIEW		
Activity	Summary	Pre-Session Prep
Activity 1: Sweet Rewards	Compare a cookie's trials in the oven to our trials in life.	You'll need sugar cookie dough, cookie cutters, baking sheets and miscellaneous baking supplies, and a Bible.
Activity 2: Faith Fall	Test your children's faith in you and learn how tests show we're growing.	You'll need a Bible.

Main Points:

—God uses trials to help us grow.

—Trials test how much we've grown.

LIFE SLOGAN: "Show and grow!"

Make it your own
In the space provided below, outline the flow and add any additional ideas to guide you through the process of conducting this family night.

Prayer & Praise Items
In the space provided below, list any items you wish to pray about or give praise for during this family night session.

Journal
In the space provided below, capture a record of any fun or meaningful things which happened during this family night session.

Session Tip

We intentionally have provided more material than we would expect to be used in a single "Family Night" session. You know your family's unique interests and life circumstances best, so feel free to adapt this lesson to meet your family members' needs. Remember, short and simple is better than long and comprehensive.

WARM-UP

Open with Prayer: Begin by having a family member pray, asking God to help everyone in the family understand more about Him through this time. After prayer, review your last lesson by asking these questions:

- **What do you remember from our last lesson?**
- **Do you remember the Life Slogan?**
- **What was one fun thing we did during our last lesson?**
- **How has what we learned last week changed your actions in the past few days?**

Share: Tonight we'll be learning about why God allows tests and trials in our lives.

ACTIVITY 1: Sweet Rewards

Point: God uses trials to help us grow.

 Supplies: You'll need sugar cookie dough, cookie cutters, baking sheets and miscellaneous baking supplies, and a Bible.

Activity: Gather around the dinner table and place a mound of cookie dough where everyone can reach it. Make cookie cutters of various shapes available as well. You might also need extra flour, rolling pins, spatulas and other assorted baking supplies.

Share: Use this dough to make any shapes you like. You can mold the dough into animal shapes, make a cookie to look like a car, use the cookie cutters, or shape the letters of your name. Anything you want!

While everyone is molding, rolling, and cutting, discuss:
- **What is a trial?** (A courtroom proceeding, a time of suffering, a painful experience, a situation you don't want to be in!)

• **What kinds of trials, or difficult situations, do you feel like you're going through right now?**

Answers will vary, but might include difficulty in a subject at school, a troubled relationship, stress at work, a missing pet, and so on. Remember that what seems like a trial to a child might not seem like a trial to an adult. Don't allow older family members to laugh off the concerns of younger ones.

When all the dough is gone and all the cookies have been shaped and placed on baking sheets, place them in the oven and bake according to the recipe.

While the cookies are baking, open your Bible to James 1:2-4 and read this passage aloud. Then discuss:

• **Why should we consider it joy when we face trials?** (Because God is testing our faith; because trials develop perseverance; because these trials help us to grow.)

• **How do you think you'll grow by going through the difficult situation you're in right now?**

• **Look back on other difficult situations you've gone through. How have you grown through these situations?**

When the cookies are done, open the oven and remove them. As they cool, have each family member place his or her hand near the opening of the oven (NOT TOUCHING ANYTHING!) to feel the heat of the air. For younger children, hold your child's hand near the open oven for a brief moment, just so they can feel the air is very hot; don't let them do it by themselves.

Age Adjustments

OLDER CHILDREN AND TEENAGERS can learn more about this principle of trials by examining the way a muscle gets stronger. Conduct several different exercises (push-ups, pull-ups, lifting, etc.) to demonstrate how muscles grow only after they've been stressed. Visit a gym or contact a trainer or coach who knows about bodybuilding. Learn how muscles must be worked and forced to endure a lot to grow stronger and bigger. Or go to the opposite extreme and visit a physical therapist to see what happens when muscles aren't used. Observe how they shrink and become useless.

How are these principles of growth and loss similar to the trials God allows us to endure? What would happen if we didn't get "flexed"? How can we have an attitude of joy during these building times?

Share: The cookie dough we placed into the oven had to endure the "trial" of baking. As you can feel, it's very hot in there. But this uncomfortable heat is what was needed to make the cookies good to eat. In the same way, God allows us to go through difficult trials because He knows this will make us into a stronger, more mature person.

Activity 2: Faith Fall

Point: Trials test how much we've grown.

 Supplies: You'll need a Bible.

Activity: Choose one child to stand in the center of the room, facing away from you.

Explain: **Keep your eyes closed and your arms folded across your chest. Keep your body straight and stiff. Now fall backward into my arms!**

Take turns doing this with each of your children. The first time they fall, catch them quickly. Then repeat the activity, this time letting them fall a little farther before catching them. Don't drop anyone! When everyone has had a turn, ask these questions:

- **Was it easy or hard to trust me to catch you? Explain your answer.**
- **Did it get easier to trust me after you knew I could and would catch you?**

Share: This was like a test where I tested to see how much you trusted me. What are other tests you've had?

- **Why do you have tests at school, in sports, or at work?** (To see how much you've learned; to see how much you already know; to see if you're ready to learn more; to see if you're ready for more responsibility.)

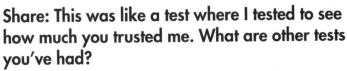 **Read** James 1:12 aloud, then ask these questions:

- **What is the reason God gives us tests?** (To see if we'll persevere; to know if we really love and trust Him.)
- **When you have tests at school or work, what's the reward?** (Good grades; a certificate; a promotion.)
- **What is the reward God gives us for tests?** (The crown of life; a closer relationship with God; joy.)

Age Adjustments

FOR YOUNGER CHILDREN, make up a fun "test" of their skills such as riding a tricycle, skipping, doing a somersault, and so on. Ask them when they learned to do these things and how. We learn to do these things through growing, through practice, and through some falls as well.

Then ask what God might be trying to help your child to do now. For example, going to sleep in a darkened room might be a problem. Help your child see that just as he or she had to practice, grow, and trust to be able to do physical things, he or she must do the same to grow in these other areas.

Share: When you fell into my arms, you passed a test of showing how much you trusted me. When you pass a test at school or work, you show how much you've learned and that you're ready for the next step of growth. In the same way, when we go through trials God has for us, we pass God's tests and grow stronger and closer to God. This lets God know we're ready to grow more and ready for Him to use us even more for His purposes.

WRAP-UP

Gather everyone in a circle and have family members take turns answering this question: **What's one thing you've learned about God today?**

Next, tell kids you've got a new "Life Slogan" you'd like to share with them.

Life Slogan: Today's Life Slogan is this: "Show and grow!" This means we SHOW God our faith when we're tested, and we GROW through the experience. Have family members repeat the slogan two or three times to help them learn it. Then encourage them to practice saying it during the week so they can talk about it at your next family night session.

Close in Prayer: Allow time for each family member to share prayer concerns and answers to prayer. Then close your time together with prayer for each concern. Thank God for making families, especially your family! Take time to thank God for each family member, mentioning one special quality you're thankful for about that person.

Remember to record prayer requests here so you can refer to them in the future as you see God answering them.

Additional Resources:

Baby Bible: Stories About Jesus by Robin Currie (ages 0-3)
Adam Raccoon and the Race to Victory Mountain by Glen Keane (ages 4-7)
In God We Trust: Stories of Faith in American History by Tim Crater and
   Ranelda Hunsicker (ages 8-12)

@ 2: That's Not Fair!

Exploring how to overcome jealousy

Scripture
- Matthew 20:1-16—Parable of the Workers in the Vineyard.
- Philippians 4:11-13—Be content in all situations.

ACTIVITY OVERVIEW		
Activity	Summary	Pre-Session Prep
Activity 1: I Want More!	Participate in an unfair activity.	You'll need money, a tape recorder or radio, and a Bible.
Activity 2: In Focus	Avoid distractions while focusing on completing a maze.	You'll need magazines or newspapers, a chair, several pads of small yellow "stickies," and a Bible.

Main Points:
—Our contentment should not be based on equality with others.
—Look at God instead of others.

LIFE SLOGAN: "It's not fair to compare!"

Make it your own

In the space provided below, outline the flow and add any additional ideas to guide you through the process of conducting this family night.

Prayer & Praise Items

In the space provided below, list any items you wish to pray about or give praise for during this family night session.

Journal

In the space provided below, capture a record of any fun or meaningful things which happened during this family night session.

Session Tip

We intentionally have provided more material than we would expect to be used in a single "Family Night" session. You know your family's unique interests and life circumstances best, so feel free to adapt this lesson to meet your family members' needs. Remember, short and simple is better than long and comprehensive.

WARM-UP

Open with Prayer: Begin by having a family member pray, asking God to help everyone in the family understand more about Him through this time. After prayer, review your last lesson by asking these questions:

- **What do you remember from our last lesson?**
- **Do you remember the Life Slogan?**
- **What was one fun thing we did during our last lesson?**
- **How has what we learned last week changed your actions in the past few days?**

Share: During our time together today we'll be learning about the problem of jealousy.

ACTIVITY 1: I Want More!

Point: Our contentment should not be based on equality with others.

Supplies: You'll need money, a tape recorder or radio, and a Bible. Note: If you don't feel comfortable using money for this activity, substitute candy bars instead, promising them to your children in amounts appropriate to the activity. For  example, the first child will receive one candy bar, the second child two, and so on.

Activity: Turn on some praise songs and listen and sing together. While the music is playing, pull your oldest child aside and privately say: **I'll give you two dollars if you can hold up your arms during the whole next song.**

When the next song begins, and while your oldest child is holding up his or her arms, pull aside your next oldest child, and privately offer this child three dollars to hold his or her arms up for the remainder of the song already playing. Continue with as many children as you have, offering each child a larger amount of money to raise his or her arms for the remainder of the song, even if this amounts to only a few moments. Remember, always keep the amount you've offered in cash private so children don't know what the others are getting.

When the song is over, have each child come to you and pay them what you've promised. Allow children to see what their siblings are getting. It won't be more than a few seconds before you start hearing "That's not fair!"

Discuss these questions:
- **Why don't you feel this is fair?** (Because others got more money than me and did less for it!)
- **Didn't I give you the amount I promised you? I delivered what I promised! Then what's not fair?** (We should have been treated equally; it's not fair that I held my arms up longer and got paid less.)
- **How do you define "fair"?**

Share: The dictionary defines fair as something that is equal to all those involved. So according to the dictionary, you're right. I didn't treat you all equally.

- How do you know when you're not being treated fairly? (When others get better treatment; when others get worse treatment.)

Share: When we compare ourselves to others, we realize we aren't always treated fairly. Then we feel jealous. Each of you was happy with what I offered to pay you for holding up your arms—until you found out what I'd paid someone else. Now you're jealous of each other.

Only One Child

If you don't have enough children to do this activity, invite a friend of your child over for the evening to participate. Be sure to offer the guest child more money than your own child. Or if you have two parents participating, pay the other adult as you would a child.

If it's just you and your child, play a game where you have the clear advantage (such as basketball if you're a lot taller, or Trivial Pursuit if you're much smarter!). After a short while, the child will begin to complain that the activity is slanted and "not fair!" At that point, continue with the Bible story and discussion that follows.

• How does comparing ourselves to others destroy our contentment? (We see others being treated differently than we are; we want what others have; we are jealous of others.)

Share: Jesus told a story very similar to the situation we have right here. Let's read it in Matthew 20:1-16.

Read Matthew 20:1-16 aloud, then discuss:

• **How is this story like our activity and the discussion we're having about fairness?** (The workers all got paid the same even though some worked all day and some only worked an hour; the workers who worked longer complained about the situation not being fair.)

• **How would you have felt if you were one of the last people hired, who got as much as the people who had worked all day?** ("Wow! This guy is generous! I don't deserve this!")

• **What about the men who worked all day? How did they feel?** ("I got cheated! I should have gotten more! I'm jealous!")

• **What did Jesus want people to learn from this story?** (God can give gifts to anyone He wants; God is generous; God is in control of who gets much and who gets little.)

• **What do you think verse 16 means when it says the last will be first and the first will be last?** (People with little may be honored greatly later; people who have a lot may someday have nothing; those who serve now will be rewarded later.)

• **What has God promised you?** (Forgiveness of my sins; an eternal home in heaven; a relationship with God.)

Share: It's true, most situations in life aren't fair, and sometimes this makes us feel jealous of others. You might not realize it now, but if you compare yourself to others in the world, you're one of those getting

Age Adjustments

FOR OLDER CHILDREN AND TEENS, consider examples of those who are last going first or those who are first going last. Together, research people who have had little in the way of possessions, or who have been treated poorly, and then have later received great honors. For example, Mother Teresa lived a life of service and poverty, yet because of her example, she won many great awards.

Or consider kings, very wealthy people, or others like them who have had a lot of money or power but been reduced to nothing. What about celebrities who get a lot of money and attention but are so unhappy without God that they turn to drugs, alcohol, and maybe even suicide? What about rulers who have treated their followers poorly and then been "dethroned" and banished from their countries? How are these people examples of Matthew 20:16? How did the unfairness work out in the end?

FOR ALL AGES, consider how unfair our lives must seem to children in other countries. In fact, many children in our own country live in poverty, without parents, with abuse, with discrimination, without enough food, and so on. What place do we have to complain? Why do we complain when others have more than us, but ignore the situations where others have less than us?

more than your fair share! There are a lot of children jealous of you.

What we have and don't have is in God's control. He gives and takes away according to His plans. We don't know all of God's plans, or the outcome of God's plans, so we should be content in our circumstances and not complain about being treated unfairly!

ACTIVITY 2: In Focus

Point: Look at God instead of others.

 Supplies: You'll need magazines or newspapers, a chair, several pads of small yellow "stickies," and a Bible.

Share: Let me read a passage to you about being content.

Read Philippians 4:11-13 aloud, then ask these questions:

- **What do you think was Paul's "secret" to not being jealous of others?** (To be content with a little or a lot)
- **Do you know much about Paul and what was happening in his life when he wrote this?** (At one time he had been rich and powerful. Now he was in jail because of his belief in Jesus. If this was us, we'd be complaining and unhappy. But Paul was content because he knew God was in control.)
- **How do we put this practice of contentment into our own lives?** (By being thankful for what we DO have; by focusing on God instead of possessions, power, popularity, or other things.)

Activity: Have family members help you make a maze on the floor of your living room or family room with magazines or newspapers forming the borders of the maze. When you're looking at the floor, it's easy to see the path to follow, but when you're looking up, it is hard to see. Then have one child stand on a chair. Have another family member take the challenge to go through the maze without touching a newspaper or magazine. This might sound easy enough, but here are the rules:

- The person going through the maze must always keep his or her eyes on the person on the chair.

- The person on the chair is the only one who can give true directions.
- Other family members can try to distract the maze walker, but cannot poke, tickle, push, or otherwise bodily move them from the path they are following.
- All other family members get pads of yellow "sticky" (Post-It) notes. Whenever they see the maze walker taking his or her eyes off the person on the chair (such as looking down or glancing aside), those with stickies can place one of them onto the maze walker.

The goal is to let each family member take a turn being the person on the chair and being the person going through the maze. Then see how well each person has done (see who has the fewest stickies stuck to them!).

 Consider these questions:

- **What does this have to do with being content instead of being jealous?** (We should be looking to God for direction instead of looking about to see what others are doing; when people distract us by telling us what they have or by comparing themselves to us, we aren't looking at God.)
- **What are distractions that keep us from looking at God?** (Seeing how much other people make at their jobs; wishing for more things; spending time on unimportant things; being angry or jealous of others.)

Age Adjustments

CHILDREN OF ALL AGES (even adults!) can learn more about contentment by making lists of what we do have. Material things are easy to think of (a home, bicycle, car, and so on), as are family members (Grandma, Aunt Betty, etc.). Then move beyond this by thinking of other blessings, such as hope, peace, citizenship in a land of many freedoms, enough food, prayer, relationship with God, and more. You might be surprised how long the list becomes when you count your blessing!

Share: Paul knew that God would provide what he truly needed. Paul knew the most important thing for him to do was to focus on doing what God wanted, to focus on his relationship with God. If we focus on God instead of worrying about who has more toys than us, who has more money than us, who has more power than us, and so on, these other things won't matter. When we're busy comparing ourselves to others and seeing how unfair life is, we're not looking at God. We need to be content with what God has given us.

WRAP-UP

Gather everyone in a circle and have family members take turns answering this question: **What's one thing you've learned**

about God today?

Next, tell kids you've got a new "Life Slogan" you'd like to share with them.

Life Slogan: Today's Life Slogan is this: "It's not fair to compare!" Have family members repeat the slogan two or three times to help them learn it. Then encourage them to practice saying it during the week so they can talk about it at your next family night session.

Close in Prayer: Allow time for each family member to share prayer concerns and answers to prayer. Then close your time together with prayer for each concern. Thank God for making families, especially your family! Take time to thank God for each family member, mentioning one special quality you're thankful for about that person.

Remember to record prayer requests here so you can refer to them in the future as you see God answering them.

Additional Resources:

The Children's Discovery Bible by Charlene Heibert (ages 4-7)
The Picture Bible by Iva Hoth (ages 8-12)

3: The Pain of Persecution

Exploring what persecution is and how to deal with it

Scripture
- Matthew 5:11-12, 44—Rejoice when persecuted and pray for your enemies.
- Romans 12:14—Bless those who persecute you.
- 1 Corinthians 4:12—Endure persecution.

ACTIVITY OVERVIEW

Activity	Summary	Pre-Session Prep
Activity 1: The Hiding Place	Secretly meet as persecuted Christians might meet.	You'll need notes as described in the lesson, a Bible, a candle or flashlight, and a dark, small space to meet.
Activity 2: Agony of da' Feet	Experience pain while striving for a reward.	You'll need a bucket, a bag of ice, marbles, and one-dollar bills.

Main Points:

—We should pray, endure, and be glad when we're persecuted.

—We can endure persecution when we look to the reward.

LIFE SLOGAN: "PEG the opposition when faced with persecution."

Make it your own
In the space provided below, outline the flow and add any additional ideas to guide you through the process of conducting this family night.

Prayer & Praise Items
In the space provided below, list any items you wish to pray about or give praise for during this family night session.

Journal
In the space provided below, capture a record of any fun or meaningful things which happened during this family night session.

Session Tip

We intentionally have provided more material than we would expect to be used in a single "Family Night" session. You know your family's unique interests and life circumstances best, so feel free to adapt this lesson to meet your family members' needs. Remember, short and simple is better than long and comprehensive.

 ### WARM-UP

Open with Prayer: Begin by having a family member pray, asking God to help everyone in the family understand more about Him through this time. After prayer, review your last lesson by asking these questions:

- **What do you remember from our last lesson?**
- **Do you remember the Life Slogan?**
- **What was one fun thing we did during our last lesson?**
- **How has what we learned last week changed your actions in the past few days?**

Share: You might have heard the word persecution. Today we're going to learn what this word means and what it has to do with our lives.

ACTIVITY 1: The Hiding Place

Point: We should pray, endure, and be glad when we're persecuted.

 **Supplies:** You'll need notes as described in the lesson, a Bible, a candle or flashlight, and a dark, small space, such as your home's crawl space, a musty attic, or large closet. The more dark, dusty, and cramped this location is, the better.

Activity: Prepare for this lesson by leaving secret notes throughout your home for family members to find. Begin leaving the notes the day before your family night. These notes should hint about the time and place you'll be meeting. For example, one note might read, "Attic," while another reads, "After dinner," and another specifies, "Be careful!" During this time you might also want to pull family members aside as if you've got a secret message and whisper, "Be sure no one follows you to our secret meeting!" or "Did you get the message?" Depending upon the ages of your children, you might have to be more explicit in your hints, but begin getting family members thinking that the upcoming "meeting" is a secretive affair.

On your family night, sneak away to the rendezvous spot (the closet, crawl space, or other location you've selected). Hopefully all family members will soon find you! If someone is missing, ask a child to sneak out and find the late family member and bring him or her to the secret location.

When everyone has arrived, use your candle or flashlight sparingly, explaining that you don't want to be caught and the light might give you away. [Note: Please be careful with fire in small spaces!] Speak in hushed tones as you begin your discussion.

 Whisper these questions:
- **Why do you think I've gathered you all here?**
- **Why do you think I've been so secretive?**

Share: In many parts of the world, Christians are not allowed to gather. Owning or reading a Bible is against the law. Churches as we know them don't exist. Talking to others about God can get you beaten, thrown in prison, even killed! These people must sneak to each other's homes to read the Bible together. They must share Bibles, often copying pages by hand and passing them on to another person. They might hide in small, dark places like this so that their neighbors won't know what's going on and turn them in to the government. What these people must endure is called persecution.

- **Do you know what persecution is?** (To harass, injure, annoy, embarrass, torture, or otherwise harm someone because of his or her beliefs.)
- **Have you ever been persecuted because of your belief in God and the Bible?**

Chances are, no one in your family has experienced severe persecution due to spiritual beliefs. However, encourage family members to consider times they have been treated badly because of believing in God. These might include:

- Not being allowed to pray in public schools, as well as not being allowed to have Christian clubs or activities at school.
- Teens and adults may not be allowed to talk about their faith at work as some companies believe talking about your beliefs to others is harassment of those who don't share your beliefs.

- Some employees might be required to donate to causes that go against their Christian beliefs, or be embarrassed by supervisors if they don't.
- A family member might be teased by friends for showing kindness to an unpopular person.
- You might be forced out of your crowd of friends because you won't participate in sinful activities such as shoplifting, using illegal drugs, telling dirty jokes, having premarital sex, cheating at school, and so on.

 Ask this question:

- **Why do you think God allows us to be persecuted, and what do you think you should do when you are persecuted?**

After family members have shared their thoughts, explain that you'd like to look to the Bible for some answers.

 Read Matthew 5:11-12, 44; Romans 12:14; 1 Corinthians 4:12 together, then discuss:

- **What should our attitude be when we're treated badly because of what we believe? Why?** (We should be glad; we should rejoice; we know other Christians have been persecuted as well; we know that we'll be rewarded in heaven.)
- **How are we to treat those who treat us badly?** (Pray for them; love them.)
- **What makes this hard?** (We would rather get revenge; it can hurt to be treated badly, so we get angry and want to hurt others back; movies and TV tell us it's right to be mean to those who harm us.)

Share: There are three things we should do when faced with persecution. P: The first thing we must remember is PRAY. We can love the people who hurt us without loving what they do. Hating others or getting revenge won't let them know about God.

E: The second thing to do is ENDURE persecution. Think of the suffering Jesus put up with. This can be an

Age Adjustments

The discussion in this section is too long for younger children. They will enjoy the excitement of the secret hiding place, but you can cut the discussion short for them. They can learn more about persecution of the early Christians by watching any of *The Storykeepers* videos (Focus on the Family and Zondervan Publishing House). These cartoons explore the challenges faced by the early church as they met in secret, had their families taken away, and tried to share the love and message of Jesus Christ with each other.

Older children, teenagers, and adults can learn more about persecution in the world today by reading *Their Blood Cries Out* by Paul Marshall with Lela Gilbert. Books like this one detail ways Christians are being persecuted around the world today, and raise questions as to why so little is being done about this persecution. Discuss what your family members can do. Can you write letters to politicians? send contributions to organizations fighting these injustices? make others more aware of what's happening? pray?

encouragement to us. Even if we are killed for what we believe, we know we'll have heaven before us, and no persecution can take that away from us.

G: Last of all, we can be GLAD because we know God will reward us for our faith. The suffering we might have to endure on earth is nothing compared to the glory of heaven!

When you put these all together, you get the word PEG. This can remind us of what to do when others treat us badly because of what we believe about God. PEG the opposition!

P—Pray
E—Endure
G—Glad

ACTIVITY 2: Agony of da' Feet

Point: We can endure persecution when we look to the reward.

 Supplies: You'll need a bucket, a bag of ice, marbles, and one-dollar bills. (As this activity can be wet and drippy, you'll probably want to do this outdoors or on a surface where cleanup will be easy. You might want to have some towels on hand as well.)

Activity: Have your children sit around you. Pour the marbles into the bottom of the bucket. Dump the bag of ice on top of the marbles, and pour a few cups of water into the mixture, stirring it around so the ice is very cold and melty. Then have children remove their shoes and socks.

Explain: **I'll give you one dollar for each marble you fish out of this bucket with your toes. Any volunteers?** (Note: If a dollar seems like too much to you, offer a quarter per marble.)

Let any child who volunteers go ahead and place his or her foot into the bucket and begin trying to bring out marbles. For each marble retrieved with the toes, pay that child one dollar. If any children are unwilling, don't force them to participate. They may change their minds upon seeing a brother or sister getting a few dollars!

We suggest you set a time limit of three minutes or five minutes for each child to retrieve marbles for two reasons. One, you may go broke with a daring child who seems able to withstand the torture of this activity. Setting a time limit will keep the number of marbles (and dollar bills) down. Second, this activity is honestly painful! A time limit will ease your mind if you're concerned about your child being willing to endure too much pain for a few dollars. Please don't allow your child to harm him or herself! Have a towel ready to dry off feet so that no one slips.

When each child has had the opportunity to place his or her feet into the icy bucket, discuss these questions:

- **Why were you willing to endure the pain of putting your feet into ice?** (For the money; for the reward)
- **If you weren't willing to do this, what was your reason? Would you have changed your mind for more money (like two dollars a marble)? Is there anything that could have gotten you to participate?**
- **How painful was it?**
- **If I hadn't set a time limit, how many more minutes of pain do you think you could have taken?**
- **What does this have to do with persecution?**

After family members have shared their thoughts on this question, explain: You were able to withstand the pain and suffering of this activity because you were looking beyond the pain. You were looking at the reward of the money you would get. In the same way, when others persecute us because of our belief in God and the Bible, we can look past the very real pain, whether physical or emotional, knowing that we have the reward of God's love, the reward of a relationship with God, and the reward of heaven.

Age Adjustments

Continue your discussion with OLDER CHILDREN AND TEENAGERS. Together, create an imaginary situation similar to real situations in countries where Christians are strongly persecuted. Consider what things would motivate you to withstand this great persecution. Would you be able to withstand physical pain? What about the uncertainty of knowing about the safety of your family? What if your home, job, and possessions were taken from you?

We can speculate about how strong we would be in our faith, but in the face of strong persecution, we might be stronger or weaker than we think. Take time now to pray for families just like yours that are suffering in other countries because they believe in God.

TEENAGERS AND ADULTS will be challenged in this topic of persecution by reading Paul McCusker's *Catacombs*. This novel follows the path of persecuted Christians as their government hunts them as lunatics and criminals.

WRAP-UP

Gather everyone in a circle and have family members take turns answering this question: **What's one thing you've learned about God today?**

Next, tell kids you've got a new "Life Slogan" you'd like to share with them.

Life Slogan: Today's Life Slogan is based on the words Pray, Endure, and be Glad that we learned in today's lesson. It's "PEG the opposi-

tion when faced with persecution." Have family members repeat the slogan two or three times to help them learn it. Then encourage them to practice saying it during the week so they can talk about it at your next family night session.

Close in Prayer: Allow time for each family member to share prayer concerns and answers to prayer. Then close your time together with prayer for each concern. Thank God for making families, especially your family! Take time to thank God for each family member, mentioning one special quality you're thankful for about that person.

Remember to record prayer requests here so you can refer to them in the future as you see God answering them.

Additional Resources:

The Children's Discovery Bible by Charlene Heibert (ages 4-7)
The Picture Bible by Iva Hoth (ages 8-12)

4: Keep the Change!

Exploring the importance of change in our lives

Scripture
- Ecclesiastes 3:1-8—There is a time for every kind of change in life.
- Hebrews 13:8—God never changes.
- Romans 8:28-39—God uses all situations for His purposes, and nothing can separate us from God's love.

ACTIVITY OVERVIEW		
Activity	Summary	Pre-Session Prep
Activity 1: Don't Change That!	Experience changes at the hands of others.	You'll need paper and pencils and a Bible.
Activity 2: Search for Change	Explore your home for evidence of change.	You'll need a Bible.

Main Points:

—Everything changes except for God.

—Change helps us grow and mature.

LIFE SLOGAN: "Change will come, we know. Change can help us grow!"

Make it your own

In the space provided below, outline the flow and add any additional ideas to guide you through the process of conducting this family night.

Prayer & Praise Items

In the space provided below, list any items you wish to pray about or give praise for during this family night session.

Journal

In the space provided below, capture a record of any fun or meaningful things which happened during this family night session.

Session Tip

We intentionally have provided more material than we would expect to be used in a single "Family Night" session. You know your family's unique interests and life circumstances best, so feel free to adapt this lesson to meet your family members' needs. Remember, short and simple is better than long and comprehensive.

 WARM-UP

Open with Prayer: Begin by having a family member pray, asking God to help everyone in the family understand more about Him through this time. After prayer, review your last lesson by asking these questions:

- **What do you remember from our last lesson?**
- **Do you remember the Life Slogan?**
- **What was one fun thing we did during our last lesson?**
- **How has what we learned last week changed your actions in the past few days?**

Share: Today we're going to learn about why change is important in our lives.

ACTIVITY 1: Don't Change That!

Point: Everything changes except for God.

Supplies: You'll need paper, pencils, and a Bible. Before your family time, prepare by counting out enough pieces of paper so each family member (including yourself) will have one. At the top of each page, write a title for the picture that will later be drawn there. For example, A Beautiful Bird, My Dream House, The Coolest Car Ever Made, The Pet I Wish I Could Have, The Best Bedroom Ever, and so on. Each page should have a different title at the top.

Activity: Gather your family members around the kitchen table. Give each person one of the titled pages and a pencil. Explain that each person is to draw a picture according to the title on his or her page.

After about two minutes, have everyone stop their drawing (even though they won't be done) and pass their picture to the person on their right. Have the drawing continue. After another two minutes, rotate the pictures again. Continue the rotation every two minutes until everyone has had a chance to draw on each picture. (If your family is very small, you might want to give everyone a chance to draw on each picture twice.)

When you've completed the drawings, give each one back to the person who originally started it. Take turns allowing each person to explain what he or she had in mind when they started the drawing. Then discuss:

- **How did the picture change from your original plan?**
- **Do you like the changes? Why or why not?**
- **What frustrates you about changes in life?** (Not being in control; having things turn out differently than I'd planned; being disappointed with how things change.)
- **What can be good about changes in life?** (We learn new things; we grow because of challenges; we make new friends; we become stronger people.)
- **Share a time when you planned things to go one way but changes happened and the outcome was different.**

Age Adjustments

To help YOUNGER CHILDREN think about the changes in their lives, brainstorm together all the changes that happen in a day at your home. Clothes get changed, the light changes outside, the food we eat at meals changes, television shows change, our feelings change, and so on. These changes are small and don't usually bother us. Bigger changes, such as moving to a new house, getting a new brother or sister, going on vacation, or other big changes can be harder to face because we don't always know what's going to happen because of these changes.

Use the passage in Ecclesiastes 3 as a challenge for OLDER CHILDREN AND TEENS. When is it time to be born? When is it time to die? When is it time to plant? When is it time to uproot? Continue through the passage, and consider which of these times in life we have control over and which ones we don't. How do these changes make us stronger? How do they help us mature? What do you think might be God's purpose for some of these changes?

The experiences your family shares may be good changes or bad changes. For example, a child may share about a new friend who she thought was going to be a lot of fun. But then she learned the friend couldn't be trusted because she gossiped or told lies. This changed the relationship. Another family member might share about a change in his job that he thought was going to make life a lot harder. But then he learned that he really enjoyed the challenge of the new job and was glad for the change.

• **Do you think God likes change? Why or why not?**

Share: Let's read a passage in the Bible that's all about change.

 Read Ecclesiastes 3:1-8 aloud, then discuss:
• **What does this passage say about change?** (There are times in life for every different thing; things don't stay the same; at different times in life we will have different experiences.)

Share: Change is going to happen in life whether we like it or not. Some changes are for the better, some are for the worse. Fortunately there is one thing that never changes, that we can always count on, and that we can turn to when the changes around us seem too hard. Anyone know what that is?

Hebrews 13:8 says, "Jesus Christ is the same yesterday and today and forever." God never changes. What can we always rely on in God? (God will always hear us, always love us, always be near us.)

Share: Even though we can't always control the changes around us, God is always in control and God never changes.

ACTIVITY 2: Search for Change

Point: Change helps us grow and mature.

 Supplies: You'll need a Bible.

Activity: Give family members a chal-lenge. Explain: **I'd like each of you to hunt around our house, inside or out, and come up with an example of change that is good. Bring back evi-dence of this change or be prepared to take us to the spot you've discovered. You have five minutes. Go!**

If family members are stumped, suggest looking at a tree in the backyard. What about the tree changes? What is good about this change? Or family members might find evidence of change in a fam-ily photo album. How have people changed physically? How is this good?

When everyone has returned, let each person show off what they've found as evidence of change and explain how it's good. You

might have a package of used birthday candles as evidence of changing ages, a driver's license to show change in ability and responsibility, a gray hair to show maturity that comes with age, a pacifier that was once used by a child to show the change of not needing this comfort any more, and so on.

Share: Change is all around us! Some changes are so small that we hardly notice them. Some, like moving to a new home, school, or job are so big that we feel stress about how we'll handle the change. The Bible can tell us even more about the good that can come from change.

 Read Romans 8:28-39 together, then discuss:
- **How would you summarize this passage?** (God uses all changes, whether they seem good or bad to us, for His purposes; *nothing*, not even changes, can separate us from God's love.)
- **How can this passage encourage you in times of change?** (Even if the change is hard, God is still in control and God loves me; even if I don't understand what's happening when things change, God knows what's going on and God still loves me.)

Age Adjustments

If you have YOUNG CHILDREN, go on the hunt for change as a family, or pair younger children with older children so they don't get frustrated.

Share: Just as your picture that you drew earlier changed after being touched by many hands, so we change by being touched by many lives and many circumstances. You didn't know what your picture was going to look like when it was done, and you don't know at this point what your life will look like when it's done. But God knows. Just as we were able to find evidence of good changes in and around our home, so God is putting evidence of good changes in our lives right now. Later we can look back on our lives and see how God used changes to make us stronger, more mature people.

 **WRAP-UP**
Gather everyone in a circle and have family members take turns answering this question: **What's one thing you've learned about God today?**

Next, tell kids you've got a new "Life Slogan" you'd like to share with them.

Life Slogan: Today's Life Slogan is this: "Change will come, we know. Change can help us grow!" Have family members repeat the slogan two or three times to help them learn it. Then encourage them to practice saying it during the week so they can talk about it at your next family night session.

Close in Prayer: Allow time for each family member to share prayer concerns and answers to prayer. Then close your time together with prayer for each concern. Thank God for making families, especially your family! Take time to thank God for each family member, mentioning one special quality you're thankful for about that person.

Remember to record prayer requests here so you can refer to them in the future as you see God answering them.

Additional Resources:

Face-to-Face With Women of the Bible by Nancy Simpson (ages 6+)
In God We Trust: Stories of Faith in American History by Tim Crater and Ranelda Hunsicker (ages 8-12)
Chronicles of Courage series by Dorothy Harrison (ages 8-12)
    -*A Better Tomorrow*
    -*Operation Morningstar*
    -*Gold in the Garden*

⌖ 5: God's Lending System

Exploring God's view on money

Scripture
- 1 Timothy 6:6-10—Loving money leads to evil actions.
- Psalm 24:1—Everything in the world belongs to God.
- Luke 12:13-21—Parable of the Rich Fool.

ACTIVITY OVERVIEW		
Activity	Summary	Pre-Session Prep
Activity 1: I Want More!	Experience the problem of loving money.	You'll need several rolls of coins, masking tape, and a Bible.
Activity 2: All That I Have	Take inventory of what we have and how it can be used by God.	You'll need pencils, paper, and a Bible.

Main Points:

—Loving money is wrong.

—God wants us to use what He's given us to glorify Him.

LIFE SLOGAN: "What I have God owns; it's just mine on loan."

Make it your own
In the space provided below, outline the flow and add any additional ideas to guide you through the process of conducting this family night.

Prayer & Praise Items
In the space provided below, list any items you wish to pray about or give praise for during this family night session.

Journal
In the space provided below, capture a record of any fun or meaningful things which happened during this family night session.

Session Tip

We intentionally have provided more material than we would expect to be used in a single "Family Night" session. You know your family's unique interests and life circumstances best, so feel free to adapt this lesson to meet your family members' needs. Remember, short and simple is better than long and comprehensive.

 WARM-UP

Open with Prayer: Begin by having a family member pray, asking God to help everyone in the family understand more about Him through this time. After prayer, review your last lesson by asking these questions:

- **What do you remember from our last lesson?**
- **Do you remember the Life Slogan?**
- **What was one fun thing we did during our last lesson?**
- **How has what we learned last week changed your actions in the past few days?**

Share: During our family time we're going to learn about how God wants us to use our money.

ACTIVITY 1: I Want More!

Point: Loving money is wrong.

Supplies: You'll need several rolls of coins (pennies, nickels, dimes, and quarters), masking tape, and a Bible. Place two rolls of coins in your pocket or another nearby hidden place before the activity.

Activity: Mark a line on the floor with masking tape. Have your children stand on one side of this line. Spread all the coins (except the two rolls hidden away) over the floor on the opposite side of the masking tape. For older children, spread the money over a very wide area (so they can't just scoop it up), and for younger children place the coins closer together. There should be more coins than you think they can pick up in ten seconds.

Explain: **You've got ten seconds to pick up as much of this money as you want. Go!**

After ten seconds, have everyone immediately stop collecting coins and move back to their side of the masking tape. Point out that there is still money left on the floor. Most likely your children will ask if they can have this money too.

Ask: **If I let you have all the rest of the money on the floor, will you be satisfied?**

Let children pick up the rest of the coins. Then, as they're counting their loot, pull out the two hidden rolls of coins, saying: **Looks like I forgot to put these out with the others!**

Again, your children are likely to ask if they can have these coins too! Consider these questions together:

- **I thought you said you'd be satisfied with the money I let you pick up! Why do you want more now?**
- **Why is money important to you?**
- **Is money good or bad?**

After children have expressed their thoughts on whether money is good or bad, **share: Money itself is not good or evil. It's just a bit of metal or paper. It's our attitude toward money that is either good or bad.**

- **Were you content with the first amount of money you collected in our activity? Why or why not?**
- **Were you unhappy that someone else might have gathered more money? Why or why not?**
- **Why did you want more money when it was available?**

Share: The Bible explains that money isn't bad itself. It's when we love money that we get into trouble.

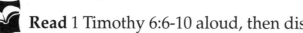

Read 1 Timothy 6:6-10 aloud, then discuss these questions:
- **What do we learn from these verses? (**We should be content with food and clothing; riches cause temptation and can lead to ruin; loving money leads to all kinds of evil.)
- **What kinds of evil things do people do when they love money?** (Steal; tell lies to get more money; kill others for their money; cheat)
- **How can loving money cause us to forget about God?** (We

Age Adjustments

Have OLDER CHILDREN AND TEENAGERS research the lives of wealthy people. Everyone from Howard Hughes to today's athletes and movie stars can be considered. Were/are these people happy? How has money brought pain to these people? Do you think of them as greedy and selfish? How have many of these men and women made money their god? How can you keep these attitudes about money from changing you in a bad way?

look at money as more important than God; we live a life of sin to get more money; we think money can solve our problems, so don't turn to God.)

Share: Loving money makes us into greedy and selfish people who forget about God. No matter how much money we have, we always want more. That's what happened in our game earlier, and that's what happens in life. We are greedy and want more, more, more. Loving money is wrong.

ACTIVITY 2: All That I Have

Point: God wants us to use what He's given us to glorify Him.

 Supplies: You'll need paper, pencils, and a Bible.

Activity: Give each person paper and a pencil, and ask: **What do you have? List what you have on this paper.**

Most family members will be quick to list their possessions. But challenge everyone to think of other things God has given you, such as family, strength, a sharp mind, a sense of humor, and so on. Help each other think of good things God has given you all to include on your lists. (Have older family members help those who cannot yet write.)

After several minutes of writing, have everyone stop and share what they've written so far. Then discuss these questions:

- **Who do these things belong to?** (Right now they belong to you, but ultimately they belong to God. God can take any of these things away at any time. What we have is on loan from God.)
- **Do you think you're doing a good job of taking care of these gifts God has loaned to you? Why or why not?**

 Read Psalm 24:1 aloud and **share: This verse says that everything is God's. Is**

Age Adjustments

Now is a great time to bring up the topic of tithing to CHILDREN OF ALL AGES. Second Corinthians 9:7 instructs us to give cheerfully to God. How can your family members begin to do that? Is everyone giving 10 percent of their earnings back to God?

An excellent resource to help children learn about tithing and saving is the "My Giving Bank" created by Rainfall and available at Christian bookstores. This bank is divided into three sections labeled Bank, Store, and Church, so children can keep their money in the places it belongs. The bank also includes information from Larry Burkett on teaching your children how to wisely manage the money God provides.

ALL FAMILY MEMBERS might enjoy playing a game of "If We Had a Million Dollars . . ." In this game your family has a million dollars to spend on others. The money cannot be spent on anyone in the family. How will you spend it? What can you do for others with this kind of gift? Now consider what you already have (which is likely a bit less than a million dollars!). How can you use this to help others?

there any way you can argue that? (No! Everything we have can be given or taken by God; when we die, we can't take anything we have with us.)

Read Luke 12:13-21 together, then ask these questions:
- **What was the attitude of this man when he had a lot of money?** (I'll store this up for myself! My life will be easy now!)
- **What happened to him?** (He died that night and couldn't take any of that wealth with him.)
- **After reading this story, what attitude do you think God wants us to have toward money?** (We shouldn't put our trust in money; money should not be loved; we should be looking for ways to please God, not ways to get more money.)

Share: God wants us to use what He's given us to please Him. Look over your list and think of ways you can use what God has given you to please Him.

Family members might consider sharing toys with friends or even giving a couple away to needy children; bringing a smile to others with a good, clean sense of humor; helping those who are behind in school with the bright mind God's given to you; leaving an anonymous gift of canned food on the doorstep of someone in need; and other similar ideas.

Share: Using what God has loaned us in these ways shares God's wealth. This is what being a steward means. We are to take care of what God gives us in the best way we know how. We can bring glory to God by using what we have as God wants us to.

WRAP-UP

Gather everyone in a circle and have family members take turns answering this question: **What's one thing you've learned about God today?**

Next, tell kids you've got a new "Life Slogan" you'd like to share with them.

Life Slogan: Today's Life Slogan is this: "What I have God owns; it's just mine on loan." Have family members repeat the slogan two or three times to help them learn it. Then encourage them to practice saying it during the week so they can talk about it at your next family night session.

Close in Prayer: Allow time for each family member to share prayer concerns and answers to prayer. Then close your time together with prayer for each concern. Thank God for making families, especially your family! Take time to thank God for each family member, mentioning one special quality you're thankful for about that person.

Remember to record prayer requests here so you can refer to them in the future as you see God answering them.

Additional Resources:

Larry Burkett's Money Matters board game (adult)
Money Matters for Kids board game (ages 8+)
My giving bank (ages 3+)
Zacheaus, the Little Man by Robin Currie (ages 1-3)
The Children's Discovery Bible by Charlene Heibert (ages 4-7)
The Picture Bible by Iva Hoth (ages 8-12)

@ 6: Knock Out!

Exploring how to keep sin out of our lives

Scripture
• Psalm 32:1-5—Sin and its guilt keep us from God and from enjoying life.
• 1 John 1:9—God will forgive us if we ask Him to.

ACTIVITY OVERVIEW		
Activity	Summary	Pre-Session Prep
The Big KO	Explore what we should do about sin in our lives.	You'll need a heavy drinking glass, a pie tin, small slips of paper, pencils, a large raw egg, a toilet paper tube, a broom, masking tape, and a Bible.

Main Point:

—God can help us knock sin out of our lives.

LIFE SLOGAN: "Knock out sin to get clean within."

Make it your own
In the space provided below, outline the flow and add any additional ideas to guide you through the process of conducting this family night.

Prayer & Praise Items
In the space provided below, list any items you wish to pray about or give praise for during this family night session.

Journal
In the space provided below, capture a record of any fun or meaningful things which happened during this family night session.

Session Tip

We intentionally have provided more material than we would expect to be used in a single "Family Night" session. You know your family's unique interests and life circumstances best, so feel free to adapt this lesson to meet your family members' needs. Remember, short and simple is better than long and comprehensive.

WARM-UP

Open with Prayer: Begin by having a family member pray, asking God to help everyone in the family understand more about Him through this time. After prayer, review your last lesson by asking these questions:

- What do you remember from our last lesson?
- Do you remember the Life Slogan?
- What was one fun thing we did during our last lesson?
- How has what we learned last week changed your actions in the past few days?

Share: During our time today we're going to learn about the problem of sin and what we can do about this problem.

ACTIVITY: The Big KO

Point: God can help us knock sin out of our lives.

Supplies: You'll need a heavy drinking glass, a pie tin (lightweight metal, not glass), small slips of paper, pencils, a large raw egg, the cardboard tube from a roll of toilet paper, a broom, masking tape, and a Bible. There are a lot of supplies for this activity, but the final effect is worth it!

Activity: Begin by asking family members to share their definitions of sin.

Share: Sin means missing the mark. If we were shooting at a target, every shot that missed the target could represent sin. A bull's-eye is what God wants, and all the shots that miss are what Satan wants.

Every time we do what God wants, we're not sinning—we're hitting the target. Every time we do what Satan wants, we are sinning—we miss the target. But what can we do about sin? That's what we're going to learn.

Give each person a few small slips of paper and a pencil.

Explain: **On these papers, write one or two sins you know you've committed recently. Maybe you've told a lie, been unkind to a family member, or done something else wrong. Write that on your paper.** (Parents can help those who cannot write yet.)

When everyone has one or two papers completed, have them place the papers facedown or once folded in the pie tin. These sins are not to be shared and discussed. What is written on the papers is between each person and God.

Share: Admitting that we have done wrong things is the first step toward dealing with sin. Admitting we've done things wrong is called confession. Confession is telling God or others that we've done something wrong. What do we do next? (Ask for forgiveness and change our actions so we don't do the same thing again.)

 Read Psalm 32:1-5 together, then discuss:
- **What happens when we don't admit we've done something wrong and try to hide what we've done?** (We feel guilty; it's hard to enjoy life; we worry that sooner or later someone will find out what we did.)
- **What happens when we ask God to forgive us for sinning?** (God forgives us! We can be free from the feelings of guilt.)

Share: God always forgives us when we ask Him to. And sometimes when we sin, we need to ask others to forgive us too. Like if you hit your brother and ask God to forgive you, God will. But you also need to ask your brother to forgive you. Then you need to change your ways, such as stop hitting your brother!

Gather in a circle and place the pie plate on the floor. Have one minute of silent prayer where everyone can ask God to forgive them for their sins. Then ask one of the children to pray and ask God to help each one to not sin in this way again.

After prayer, set the pie plate aside for later use.

Ask:
• What can we do to keep sin out of our lives?

As family members share their ideas, have one person write these on strips of masking tape, and another person place the tape on the handle of the broom. Answers might include praying, reading the Bible to know what is right and wrong; going to church and learning what actions God wants us to do; singing songs of praise to God; memorizing verses from the Bible; and so on. As family members share ideas, discuss how that idea helps us keep sin out of our lives.

Prayer places us in direct communication with God and helps us focus on God. Then we can't be focusing on doing what's wrong!

By **reading the Bible,** we can listen to God and what He wants for us, not what we want or what Satan wants.

Going to church gives us the chance to learn from other Christians. If we share areas where we're trying not to sin, they can hold us accountable.

Praising God causes us to acknowledge who God is and how holy He is. This helps us realize how much we need God in every area of our lives.

Memorizing verses from the Bible keeps God's thoughts near to us. Jesus quoted Scripture to Satan when Satan tried to get Jesus to sin.

After your discussion, explain that now's the time to see how sin can get knocked out of our lives!

Fill a heavy drinking glass half to three-quarters of the way with water. Place the glass near the edge of your kitchen table. Take the pie tin with sins in it and center it directly on the top of the water glass, but so one edge comes out over the edge of the table. Next, place the cardboard toilet paper tube in the center of the pie tin, moving the pieces of paper so the tube rests directly on the pie tin. Finally, place the large egg on top of the tube. Make sure it doesn't sit too low in the tube (place the wide end of the egg in the tube). Your demonstration is now set up. (By the way, you might also want to set up a video camera to film this. Then you can watch the action in slow motion over and over.)

Explain: **Let's say that we are the egg and the water is God. We are separated from God by sin** (the pie tin with slips of paper in it). **How can we knock sin out without touching a thing? Is it possible?**

Allow children to share their ideas on how to do this. Then **share: To knock sin out, we need to use the tools we just discussed.**

Get the broom that now has masking tape with ways to keep sin out of our lives on its handle. Place the bristles of the broom directly underneath the end of the table where the egg and glass are arranged. Bend the bristles so that you can stand on them. Firmly step on the bristles and pull the handle of the broom back toward yourself at about a 45-degree angle. You'll need to apply enough pressure that the broom handle will snap back up when you release it. When you're ready, release the handle. It will snap up and hit the pie tin that is hanging over the edge of the table, force it and the tube out of the way, and the egg will fall into the water!

For Everyone

All family members might want to take the opportunity now to ask for forgiveness from other family members. Or encourage each other to call or write a note of apology to others who you might have wronged.

We admit this is tricky, but it really does work. If you have a failed attempt, try again with a new egg. (And in the meantime you can comment on what a big mess we make when we sin as you're cleaning up the mess of the egg! Have family members share times they've made a mess of situations by sinning instead of doing what was right.)

Share: Using the ideas we had for keeping away from sin such as praying and reading the Bible (on the broom handle) knocked sin (the pie plate) out of the way and let us (the egg) fall into God's presence (the water)!

Read 1 John 1:9 aloud, then **share: When we tell God what we've done wrong and ask Him to forgive us, He does. Then we're clean and in God's presence again, just like the egg is in the water.**

If you videotaped the process, watch it again in slow motion! Or try it again with a few new eggs.

WRAP-UP

Gather everyone in a circle and have family members take turns answering this question: **What's one thing you've learned about God today?**

Next, tell kids you've got a new "Life Slogan" you'd like to share with them.

● **Life Slogan: Today's Life Slogan is this: "Knock out sin to get clean within."** Have family members repeat the slogan two or three times to help them learn it. Then encourage them to practice saying it during the week so they can talk about it at your next family night session.

Close in Prayer: Allow time for each family member to share prayer concerns and answers to prayer. Then close your time together with prayer for each concern. Thank God for making families, especially your family! Take time to thank God for each family member, mentioning one special quality you're thankful for about that person.

Remember to record prayer requests here so you can refer to them in the future as you see God answering them.

Additional Resources:

The New Kid's Choices (ages 6-12)
The New Teen Choices (ages 12-18)
Baby Bible: Stories About Jesus by Robin Currie (ages 0-3)
The Picture Bible by Iva Hoth (ages 8-12)
Following Jesus by Barry St. Clair (ages 12+)

⊚ 7: Cavity Filler

Exploring our need to have a relationship with God

Scripture
- Ecclesiastes 3:11—God has placed a longing in the hearts of people.
- Isaiah 55:1-2—God will freely give us what will satisfy our needs—Himself.

ACTIVITY OVERVIEW		
Activity	Summary	Pre-Session Prep
Activity 1: All I Need	Consider what would make us truly happy in life.	You'll need pencils, paper, and a Bible.
Activity 2: The Empty Hole	Examine ways we incorrectly try to fulfill the need in our lives.	You'll need a battery-operated doll; batteries; a dollar bill, pictures of a house, an expensive car, and a pretty woman or handsome man; and a Bible.

Main Points:
  —We all have a need in our lives.
  —Only a relationship with God can fill our need.

LIFE SLOGAN: "God is all that satisfies. Other things are lies."

Make it your own
In the space provided below, outline the flow and add any additional ideas to guide you through the process of conducting this family night.

Prayer & Praise Items
In the space provided below, list any items you wish to pray about or give praise for during this family night session.

Journal
In the space provided below, capture a record of any fun or meaningful things which happened during this family night session.

Session Tip

WARM-UP

Open with Prayer: Begin by having a family member pray, asking God to help everyone in the family understand more about Him through this time. After prayer, review your last lesson by asking these questions:

- **What do you remember from our last lesson?**
- **Do you remember the Life Slogan?**
- **What was one fun thing we did during our last lesson?**
- **How has what we learned last week changed your actions in the past few days?**

Share: In our time today we'll be exploring our need to have a relationship with God.

ACTIVITY 1: All I Need

Point: We all have a need in our lives.

Supplies: You'll need paper, pencils, and a Bible.

IF I HAD A MILLION DOLLARS I WOULD BE COMPLETELY HAPPY!

Activity: Give each person a piece of paper and a pencil. Explain that each person is to complete the sentence, "If I had _____, I would be completely happy." For example, "If I had a million dollars, I would be completely happy." Younger family members who cannot write may draw their answer in the form of a picture. Don't share your answers as you work.

After everyone (including you!) has completed their sentence, go around the family and see if others can guess what each person said would make him or her completely happy. This is a fun opportunity to see just how well you know each other!

When everyone has described what would make them happy, discuss:

- **Do you think if you had this one thing you would be completely and truly happy?**
- **How long would this happiness last before you decided you needed something else as well?**

Share: We all hope for something in life to make us happy. The Bible talks about this in Ecclesiastes 3:11.

 Read Ecclesiastes 3:11 aloud, then discuss:

- **What do you think this verse means?**
- **What do you think it means when it says God has "set eternity in the hearts of men"? (God has put a longing, a desire, or a hope in our hearts.)**

Share: God made us in His image. Part of what that means is that we have a need for relationship with God. Our next activity will help us understand this even more.

ACTIVITY 2: The Empty Hole

Point: Only a relationship with God can fill our need.

 Supplies: You'll need a doll that requires batteries; batteries for the doll; a dollar bill; pictures of a house, an expensive car, and a pretty woman or handsome man (you can cut these pictures from a magazine); and a Bible. If a doll isn't available, another battery-operated toy could be substituted. Prepare for this activity by removing the batteries from the doll and setting them aside.

Activity: Show family members the doll with the empty place where the batteries belong, then ask:

- **What does this doll need to do "the thing that it does" (such as walk, cry, laugh, or whatever)? (Batteries!)**

Share: We all know it needs batteries. There is a hole here in the doll

made specifically for batteries. But I wonder if anything else can make this doll work.

- **What happens when I put money in the battery compartment?** Place the dollar bill into the battery opening. (Nothing happens. The doll needs batteries.)
- **What happens if I give this doll a house? A nice car? A handsome boyfriend?** Place the pictures of these items in the battery compartment as you ask each question.

Share: Nothing happens because this doll was made to need batteries.

Place the batteries in the doll and demonstrate how she now functions properly.

 Ask:
- **How is this like the need we have?** (We all have a need that God put in us.)

Share: The need we have is not for batteries. The need we have is for a relationship with God. Everyone has this need, but not everyone looks to God to fill this need. A lot of people try to stuff other things in their lives to fill this need, just as we tried to stuff other things into the doll's battery compartment. What things do people try to use to fill this need?

There are many answers to this question. Here are a few your family might consider:

People: We look for friends, boyfriends, girlfriends, husbands, and wives to fill this need. Or we think that if we're popular enough, this need will be met. But people are not perfect and will never meet all your needs and expectations. And no one can stay popular forever. Trying to please others all the time won't fill your need.

Places: We try to buy nice houses and take wonderful vacations to fill our need. But there is always a bigger house or a better vacation, so we can never be satisfied.

Things: We try to use money, an important job, a new bike, a better car, and other things to fill this need. But we never have enough. Others have things better than we do. What we have can't fill this need.

Drugs: Sadly, many people look to drugs and alcohol to fill this need. They feel so empty they think they can only find happiness through chemicals. But these leave them worse off than when they started. Such substances ruin our minds and our lives and never fill the need for God.

Activities: Some people get busy trying to save animals, protect lost children, preserve the environment, or help others in some way. These are important activities that make us feel like we're helping others, but they still can't fill the need we have for God.

Share: The Bible tells us the only thing that can fill this hole in our lives is a relationship with God. The whole reason Jesus came to earth, died on the cross, and rose again was so that we could have a relationship with God. The Bible tells us over and over that God loves us and wants us to draw close to Him, to have a relationship with Him. The Bible has a message to those who are trying to stuff cars, houses, friends and other things into the hole made for God.

 Read Isaiah 55:1-2 aloud, then discuss this question:
- **What are these verses saying?**

Age Adjustments

For YOUNGER CHILDREN, the concept of filling their lives with cars and houses won't make sense. Instead, try to stuff other toys into the battery compartment of the doll. Every child wants more toys, and it seems they never have enough!

Have OLDER CHILDREN AND TEENAGERS discuss other ways people try to fill their needs today. Examine the lives of current celebrities to see how they try to fill their lives. What messages do we get from the media about what will fill our needs? Why do you think so many people turn to cults to fill their needs? How do these false methods destroy lives?

For CHILDREN OF ALL AGES, this lesson provides a perfect opportunity to bring up the topic of salvation with your children. For more help on this, refer to "Leading Your Child to Christ" on page 106 of this book.

After family members have expressed their thoughts, explain: **This verse starts off saying that if you are thirsty, come and eat and drink for free. Don't spend money on something that isn't food. Don't work hard for something that won't satisfy you. God is saying He knows we have a need, and He will fill that need in our lives for free. We shouldn't waste our time and money chasing after things that won't fill that need. What we need is a relationship with God, and that's free!**

Turn the doll back on and share: Just as this doll has a hole in her that can only be filled with batteries, so we have a hole in us that can only be filled by a relationship with God.

WRAP-UP

Gather everyone in a circle and have family members take turns answering this question: **What's one thing you've learned about God today?**

Next, tell kids you've got a new "Life Slogan" you'd like to share with them.

Life Slogan: Today's Life Slogan is this: "God is all that satisfies. Other things are lies." Have family members repeat the slogan two or three times to help them learn it. Then encourage them to practice saying it during the week so they can talk about it at your next family night session.

Close in Prayer: Allow time for each family member to share prayer concerns and answers to prayer. Then close your time together with prayer for each concern. Thank God for making families, especially your family! Take time to thank God for each family member, mentioning one special quality you're thankful for about that person.

Remember to record prayer requests here so you can refer to them in the future as you see God answering them.

Additional Resources:

Bible Words About Happiness for Children by Lois Rock (ages 4-7)
A Better Tomorrow? by Dorothy Harrison (ages 8-12)

@ 8:Trapped!

Exploring Satan's traps of sin and how to avoid being caught in them

Scripture
- Luke 4:1-13—Jesus is tempted by Satan.
- Psalm 119:9-11—Hide God's Word in your heart to avoid sin.
- Proverbs 3:5-6—Look to God for guidance.

ACTIVITY OVERVIEW		
Activity	Summary	Pre-Session Prep
Activity 1: Gotcha!	Learn about traps for animals and traps for humans.	You'll need a cardboard box, string, a stick, a small ball, and a Bible.
Activity 2: Tricks and Traps	Be guided through a maze of traps just as God guides us.	You'll need mousetraps, a pencil, a blindfold, and a Bible.

Main Points:

> —Satan is always looking for ways to trap us.

> —God can guide us away from Satan's traps.

LIFE SLOGAN: "If it looks really good, ask God if you should!"

Make it your own

In the space provided below, outline the flow and add any additional ideas to guide you through the process of conducting this family night.

Prayer & Praise Items

In the space provided below, list any items you wish to pray about or give praise for during this family night session.

Journal

In the space provided below, capture a record of any fun or meaningful things which happened during this family night session.

Session Tip

We intentionally have provided more material than we would expect to be used in a single "Family Night" session. You know your family's unique interests and life circumstances best, so feel free to adapt this lesson to meet your family members' needs. Remember, short and simple is better than long and comprehensive.

WARM-UP

Open with Prayer: Begin by having a family member pray, asking God to help everyone in the family understand more about Him through this time. After prayer, review your last lesson by asking these questions:

- **What do you remember from our last lesson?**
- **Do you remember the Life Slogan?**
- **What was one fun thing we did during our last lesson?**
- **How has what we learned last week changed your actions in the past few days?**

Share: Our time today will be spent learning about the traps of life.

ACTIVITY 1: Gotcha!

Point: Satan is always looking for ways to trap us.

Supplies: You'll need a cardboard box (such as a shoe box), string, a stick, a small ball, and a Bible.

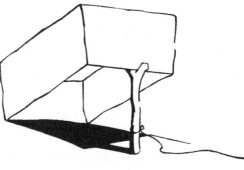

Activity: Using a cardboard box, string, and stick, make a simple trap. Tie a length of string, at least three feet long, to the stick. Then use the stick to prop up one side of the cardboard box. When the string is pulled, the stick should fall down, allowing the box to drop and trap anything underneath it.

Give the string to one family member, and a small ball to another family member. Have the person with the ball roll it under the trap and see if the person holding the string is quick enough to pull out the stick and trap the ball. Take turns rolling the ball and pulling the stick until everyone has had a chance to play.

Share: There are three kinds of traps. Can you guess what they are?

After family members have guessed, explain: **The three kinds are enclosing traps, arresting traps, and killing traps. An enclosing trap catches an animal without hurting it. An arresting trap grips the animal but does not kill it. A killing trap grips the animal, then kills it with a blow.**

 Discuss these questions:
- **What kind of trap did we make with our box?** (An enclosing trap)
- **What do you think are the most important things to remember when you're setting a trap?** (Disguise the trap so the animal can't tell it's there, and put appropriate bait in it to draw the animal to the trap.)

Share: People who use traps are careful to put food or other bait into the traps so animals will want to come close enough. They often disguise the trap with leaves or branches, and sometimes put special sprays on or around the traps so the animals can't detect humans have been there by the smell.

People aren't the only ones setting traps. Satan is busy setting his own traps to catch us! They aren't traps where he tries to catch our leg or snag us in a net. Satan is trying to trap us in sin and lead us away from God. Satan even tried to trap Jesus! Let's read about that in the Bible.

 Read Luke 4:1-13 together, then discuss:
- **What kind of "bait" did Satan use in trying to trap Jesus in sin?** (Hunger; power; riches; trying to get Jesus to prove He was God.)
- **How did Satan disguise his traps?** (He made it look like he was concerned about Jesus being hungry; he even quoted verses from the Bible; he placed temptation right in front of Jesus.)
- **How did Jesus resist the temptation to get ensnared in these traps?** (He used verses from the Bible to guide Him.)
- **What can Satan use to tempt us today? What can he use as bait? How would we be trapped?**

There are many answers to these questions. Some you and your

family might consider include:

• Satan can tempt us with our **pride**. The bait could be wanting to impress our friends. A teenager might try to impress friends by smoking, drinking, or using drugs. Then this person is trapped in a lifestyle with unhealthy addictions.

• Satan can tempt us with our desire for **power**. The bait could be a big promotion at work. A father might want to have more power and prestige at his office, plus more money, so he accepts a job that will give him these things. But then he's trapped in a lifestyle where he has no time for his family, church, or God.

• Satan can tempt us using our **physical desires**. The bait can be too much food, things we see in advertisements, and so on. The trap might be overeating, stealing, and on and on.

Share: Satan looks for ways he can trap us. Sometimes these things start out looking good to us. But Satan can twist even a good thing and make it into something bad. Let's learn how we can avoid these traps.

Age Adjustments

For SMALL CHILDREN, make another fun trap by spreading a blanket on the floor. Have two or more adults or teenagers hold the four corners of the blankets. When a small child walks across the blanket, pull up the four corners and catch the child. A bit of swinging around in the trap is fun too!

Also, the concept of spiritual entrapment might be too abstract for YOUNG CHILDREN. Avoid the drugs, power at work, and sex traps. Instead, focus on traps such as fighting over a toy, hitting siblings, acting selfishly, and other behaviors young children understand.

With OLDER CHILDREN AND TEENAGERS, discuss ways Satan disguises his traps. One way is to take a good thing and twist it into something bad. For example, sex in marriage is a good thing. But sex outside of marriage, or getting involved in pornography, is an evil twist on what God created for good. Another example is music, which can be uplifting and beautiful. But Satan has twisted this with profane lyrics and singers whose lives go against everything of God. What other examples can you think of? Which of these traps do you think Satan is most likely to use on you?

Heritage
BUILDERS

Point: God can guide us away from Satan's traps.

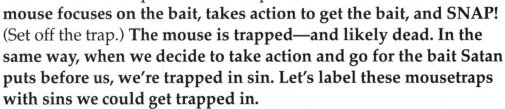

Supplies: You'll need ten or more inexpensive mousetraps, a pencil, a blindfold, and a Bible.

Activity: Set a mousetrap according to the manufacturer's directions. Use a pencil to touch the spring and set off the trap. Discuss what kind of trap this is (either an arresting trap or a killing trap, depending on how the mouse is positioned in the trap).

Explain: **A bit of food is the bait that draws a mouse to this trap.** (Show where the food would be placed in the trap.) **The mouse focuses on the bait, takes action to get the bait, and SNAP!** (Set off the trap.) **The mouse is trapped—and likely dead. In the same way, when we decide to take action and go for the bait Satan puts before us, we're trapped in sin. Let's label these mousetraps with sins we could get trapped in.**

On each mousetrap, write a different sin your family members might get trapped in. Consider sins you are likely to commit, such as gossip, selfishness, greed, lying, and so on. Most likely your family members aren't going to be involved in murder or bank robbery, so don't include those on your traps.

When the traps are labeled, place them randomly around the room. Have all the children sit on the couch or another safe place while you set each trap.

Bring out the blindfold and explain: **Now, I've got this blindfold here, and I want you all to take off your shoes and socks. I'll blindfold you and have you walk around the room. Hopefully you won't step on any traps.**

Of course your children will protest. Being snapped with a trap is very painful, especially on little toes! The object here is to get your children to protest. Don't let them actually do this!

Share: Okay, I won't ask you to walk through alone. I'll guide you.

Blindfold one of your children, and guide him or her around the room, being careful to avoid every trap. Take turns until all your

children have had a chance to participate. If you are brave and trusting, let your children guide you around the room as well. Afterward, carefully spring all the traps with a pencil and put them away.
Then discuss:

- **Why did you let me lead you around the room?** (You knew where the traps were; you could see the traps.)
- **How is this like avoiding Satan's traps?** (We need someone to guide us; we need someone who sees the traps; we need to be able to know what the traps are.)
- **What kinds of things help us see and avoid Satan's traps?** (Reading the Bible; praying; listening to parents, teachers, pastors, and others God has put in authority over us because they might be able to see traps we don't see.)

Share: When Jesus was tempted by Satan, He quoted the Bible. The Bible tells us what is right for us to do and what is wrong. Our relationship with God helps us keep away from traps too. Listen to what the Bible says.

 Read Psalm 119:9-11 and Proverbs 3:5-6 aloud, then talk about these questions:

- **How do we hide God's Word in our hearts?** (By reading it a lot; by memorizing it.)
- **How do we acknowledge God?** (Ask God for guidance; trust God to know what is best for our lives.)

Share: Just as you could depend on me to guide you away from the mousetraps, so you can depend on God and God's Word to guide you away from Satan's traps. If we are faithful to read our Bibles and obey God, we won't be trapped in sin.

WRAP-UP

Gather everyone in a circle and have family members take turns answering this question: **What's one thing you've learned about God today?**

Next, tell kids you've got a new "Life Slogan" you'd like to share with them.

Age Adjustments

For OLDER CHILDREN AND TEENAGERS, continue this activity with a challenge to look up Bible verses relating to each sin you wrote on the mousetraps. Use a concordance or Bible dictionary to help you. If you can't find a verse relating to a specific sin, look for a more general verse that might also apply. For example, there's no verse in the Bible about graphic music, but Philippians 4:8 guides us to think about things that are pure and excellent. Do these songs qualify? Could memorizing some of these verses help family members avoid traps of sin? Think of ways to encourage each other to learn some of these verses as a guard and guide against Satan's traps.

Life Slogan: Today's Life Slogan is this: "If it looks really good, ask God if you should!" Have family members repeat the slogan two or three times to help them learn it. Then encourage them to practice saying it during the week so they can talk about it at your next family night session.

Close in Prayer: Allow time for each family member to share prayer concerns and answers to prayer. Then close your time together with prayer for each concern. Thank God for making families, especially your family! Take time to thank God for each family member, mentioning one special quality you're thankful for about that person.

Remember to record prayer requests here so you can refer to them in the future as you see God answering them.

Additional Resources:

New Teen Choices (ages 12-18)
New Kid's Choices (ages 6-12)
The Ten Commandments for Children by Lois Rock (ages 4-7)

9: Now Hear This!

Exploring the importance of listening

Scripture
- Proverbs 1:5, 8-9; and 4:1—The wise listen to learn.
- James 1:19—Be quick to listen and slow to speak.

ACTIVITY OVERVIEW		
Activity	Summary	Pre-Session Prep
Activity 1: Lesson in Listening	Learn a new skill through listening.	You'll need a Bible and supplies (see the activity).
Activity 2: Slow Zone	Practice speed speech and its problems.	You'll need a Bible.

Main Points:

—We must listen to learn.

—We need to think before we speak.

LIFE SLOGAN: "Slow to speak and quick to listen helps us learn what we've been missin'!"

Make it your own
In the space provided below, outline the flow and add any additional ideas to guide you through the process of conducting this family night.

Prayer & Praise Items
In the space provided below, list any items you wish to pray about or give praise for during this family night session.

Journal
In the space provided below, capture a record of any fun or meaningful things which happened during this family night session.

Session Tip

We intentionally have provided more material than we would expect to be used in a single "Family Night" session. You know your family's unique interests and life circumstances best, so feel free to adapt this lesson to meet your family members' needs. Remember, short and simple is better than long and comprehensive.

WARM-UP

Open with Prayer: Begin by having a family member pray, asking God to help everyone in the family understand more about Him through this time. After prayer, review your last lesson by asking these questions:

- **What do you remember from our last lesson?**
- **Do you remember the Life Slogan?**
- **What was one fun thing we did during our last lesson?**
- **How has what we learned last week changed your actions in the past few days?**

Share: This lesson will help us understand why listening is so important.

ACTIVITY 1: Lesson in Listening

Point: We must listen to learn.

Supplies: You'll need a Bible and whatever items are necessary for the task you choose in the activity.

Activity: Explain to your family that you'd like to teach them a special skill you have. Let the ages and interests of your children, as well as your own special abilities, determine what this skill is. You might teach them something as simple as how to fold and create a paper airplane, then have contests seeing who can fly theirs the farthest. Or you might teach family members to bake a pie, and let each person create a small tart with your guidance. Other ideas you might consider:

- How to use a fishing pole

- How to make a small pillow using the sewing machine
- How to draw with charcoal pencils
- How to change a tire on the car
- How to make any kind of craft you enjoy

Explain the instructions clearly to your family, and have fun taking turns or working together to learn this new skill or lesson. You can make this an outing (as in the case of the fishing pole) or a time where everyone ends up creating something (as with a pillow or craft).

When you've finished with the lesson, discuss these questions:

- **In order to learn this skill, what did you have to do?** (Pay attention; listen; try to understand; ask questions.)
- **How is this like the ways God teaches us?** (We have to listen to God, pay attention to what we learn from the Bible or from church; we need to ask questions to understand.)

Share: The Bible stresses one important way we can learn.

 Read Proverbs 1:5, 8-9; and 4:1 aloud, then discuss:

- **What do these verses mention in common?** (Listening)
- **What are the rewards of listening?** (Added learning; guidance; understanding)
- **What are we supposed to be listening for?** (Guidance; lessons we should learn)

Share: Listening helps us learn. It helps us to learn in school, in church, in our home, everywhere! Listening helps us understand what God

Age Adjustments

CHILDREN will enjoy playing "Telephone" to further understand the importance of listening. Sit in a circle. Begin by whispering a message into the ear of the person next to you. Make the message easier if you have younger children, and harder or longer if you have older children. The person who just heard the message then whispers what he or she heard into the ear of the next person, and so on around the circle. At the end of the circuit, have the last person tell aloud what he or she heard. Compare this to what was actually said at the beginning of the circle. How does this happen in real life? How do messages get distorted? How do channels of communication get mixed up? How can listening and asking questions help avoid these problems?

expects from us and what others are trying to communicate. Some ways we can listen to God are by reading the Bible, by being quiet in times of prayer, and by listening to wise people God has placed in our lives. It's important we listen just as you listened when we were learning a new skill. We must listen to learn.

ACTIVITY 2: Slow Zone

Point: We need to think before we speak.

 Supplies: You'll need a Bible.

Share: Listening is very important. But we can't just listen in life. We have to talk as well. This game will help us learn something important about talking.

Think of a song, verse, or nursery rhyme your whole family knows. For this lesson we'll use the example of Humpty Dumpty, but you can substitute anything else you like.

Tell your family the title of the rhyme you'll be saying together. Then sit in a circle and start the rhyme by saying one word. The next person says the second word, the third person the third word, and so on. When you've gone around the circle, continue the poem without stopping. For example,

Mom: Humpty
Ben: Dumpty
Joel: sat
Lisa: on
Dad: a
Mom: wall.
Ben: Humpty . . . (and so on)

After you've said it through one time like this, pick up speed and go as fast as you can around the circle. See how many mistakes you make! If you can do the rhyme perfectly at fast speed, choose a harder rhyme or poem.

Then catch your breath and discuss these questions:

• **Was it easy or hard for you to recite the poem like this? Why?**

• **What happens when we're trying to talk fast and not think**

about the words? (We get mixed up; we say the wrong thing.)

- **Does it ever happen to you in life that you don't think about what you're saying, then realize you've hurt someone's feelings or called someone a mean name or something else bad? When that happens, how do you feel?**

Share: Once words are out of our mouths, we can't take them back. There's a story of a woman who had said mean things about others and then felt sorry. She asked a wise man what she should do. He told her to put a feather on the doorstep of each person she'd said something mean about. She did this. Then he told her to go pick the feathers back up. But when she returned to their homes, the feathers had blown away. The wise man told the woman, "The feathers are gone and you can never get them back. In the same way, words that have come out of your mouth are gone. You can never get them back either."

When we say something mean or wrong, we can apologize and say we're sorry, but what we've said still hurts others.

- **How can we avoid hurting people with our words?** (Don't say mean things; think about what we say before we speak.)

 Read James 1:19 together and discuss:

- **What should we first be doing?** (Listening; being quick to listen.)
- **How are we quick to listen?** (It means to pay attention to what others say without thinking about your answer; *hear* others; our first goal should be to hear what someone is saying.)
- **Then what are we to do?** (Be slow to speak.)
- **What does this mean?** (Take time to think about what we're going to say before we say it.)
- **Why should we be slow to anger too?** (If we're listening to what someone is saying, and carefully choosing our words in reply, we're less likely to hurt their feelings or get our feelings hurt. This helps us slow down our anger when we disagree.)

Share: God doesn't want us to spend our lives without learning and just fighting with others or hurting other people's feelings. We have to listen to what people say, and we have to choose carefully what we say to others. Words that hurt others are not honoring to God. We should use our words to build others up instead of tear them down.

Take time now to share words of encouragement with each other. Have one family member sit in the center of the circle and let everyone else share one or two things they like about that person. The person in the middle has to listen! Take turns so each person gets a chance to be in the middle of the circle.

Challenge family members to listen closely to others and hear what they're saying. You might even try having everyone count to ten before they answer others for one day.

WRAP-UP

Gather everyone in a circle and have family members take turns answering this question: **What's one thing you've learned about God today?**

Next, tell kids you've got a new "Life Slogan" you'd like to share with them.

Life Slogan: Today's Life Slogan is this: "Slow to speak and quick to listen help us learn what we've been missin'!" Have family members repeat the slogan two or three times to help them learn it. Then encourage them to practice saying it during the week so they can talk about it at your next family night session.

Close in Prayer: Allow time for each family member to share prayer concerns and answers to prayer. Then close your time together with prayer for each concern. Thank God for making families, especially your family! Take time to thank God for each family member, mentioning one special quality you're thankful for about that person.

Remember to record prayer requests here so you can refer to them in the future as you see God answering them.

Additional Resources:

Jesus and the Big Catch by Jeannie Harmon (ages 1-3)
Adam Raccoon and the Flying Machine by Glen Keane (ages 4-7)
Time Out! by Janet Holm McHenry (ages 8-10)

Age Adjustments

For OLDER CHILDREN AND TEENAGERS, have family members (including parents) write down what they do when they get angry. Slam doors? Sit quietly and stew? Shout? Then have others share how they see each person act when he or she is angry. Take turns expressing your thoughts. This is a delicate topic as no one wants to feel picked on. Be kind as you share your observations with each other. Focus on listening! Then let each person tell what he or she does when he or she is angry. How do what is written and what others see compare? How are these actions good or bad? What are better ways of controlling your emotions? Pray together for God's strength to be slow in becoming angry.

10: The True Treasure

Exploring why we should seek the truth

Scripture
• Romans 1:25—Exchanging God's truth for lies.
• Proverbs 2:1-5—Seek after truth and wisdom as if they were treasure.

ACTIVITY OVERVIEW		
Activity	Summary	Pre-Session Prep
Activity 1: Fool's Gold	Follow easy clues to a false treasure.	You'll need an empty box and clues as described in the lesson.
Activity 2: The Real McCoy	Follow harder clues to a true treasure.	You'll need a box of candy, clues as described in the lesson, and a Bible.

Main Points:

—It's easy to follow a lie, but it leads to disappointment.
—It is better to follow the truth, even when it's harder.

LIFE SLOGAN: "It's best for you to seek what's true!"

Make it your own
In the space provided below, outline the flow and add any additional ideas to guide you through the process of conducting this family night.

Prayer & Praise Items
In the space provided below, list any items you wish to pray about or give praise for during this family night session.

Journal
In the space provided below, capture a record of any fun or meaningful things which happened during this family night session.

WARM-UP

Open with Prayer: Begin by having a family member pray, asking God to help everyone in the family understand more about Him through this time. After prayer, review your last lesson by asking these questions:

- **What do you remember from our last lesson?**
- **Do you remember the Life Slogan?**
- **What was one fun thing we did during our last lesson?**
- **How has what we learned last week changed your actions in the past few days?**

Share: During our family time we're going to learn why it's important to seek after what's true.

ACTIVITY 1: Fool's Gold

Point: It's easy to follow a lie, but it leads to disappointment.

Supplies: You'll need a set of clues as described in the lesson and an empty box.

Activity: Prepare for this activity by hiding the empty box, then writing a few simple clues to help your children find the box. The clues should be very easy, such as "Look in the mailbox," where they find a clue that says, "Look under Mom's pillow," and so on. Use only three or four clues to lead to the box.

When you're ready, gather your family and excitedly explain that you've hidden a treasure for them to find! Give them the first clue, and watch them happily race around to find the box. Be sure to have children take turns reading the clues or going to the place where the next clue is hidden. This will keep younger or slower children from tears when they feel like they never got a turn or a chance to be involved.

When they've discovered the empty treasure, sit down together and ask your children to share how they're feeling about what they found (or should we say, didn't find!). Let your children know you're disappointed too, and share in their frustrations and feelings of "No fair!" and "What a rip off!"

Then explain: **It seems to me you've been following a false map. Those clues were a bunch of lies! I have some different clues. Why don't you try them instead?**

Move on to the next activity.

Variation: If you like, fill the box with trash, such as crumpled newspaper or empty candy wrappers, or simply put a note in the box saying something like "You've been tricked!" or "Fool's Gold!"

ACTIVITY 2: The Real McCoy

Point: It is better to follow the truth, even when it's harder.

 Supplies: You'll need a second set of clues as described in this lesson, a box of candy or other treats your children will enjoy, and a Bible.

Activity: Before your family time, prepare by hiding the box of candy and writing clues leading to this treasure. Be sure none of the hiding places for clues are the same places you used in the first activity. You might also want to use a different color of paper for these clues to further differentiate them from the first set of clues. For this treasure hunt, make the clues more difficult to follow, and prepare more clues. The object is to make this hunt harder all around. For example, "One of Ryan's chores" might lead to several places before children find the clue taped to the dog food. Or "This gets opened at noon each day" might eventually lead your children to one of their lunch boxes where you've placed the next clue. Let the ages of your children determine how hard the clues should be (you don't want them to be *impossible*), keeping in mind that this hunt should be a challenge.

After children have gone through the first activity and come up empty-handed, give them the first clue for this second hunt and set them to work. Again, be sure to have children take turns in reading or finding clues to keep from having quarrels. If you absolutely must, you can give hints on hard clues, but try to let kids work them out as much as possible.

When kids have finally found the treasure of the box of candy,

rejoice with them and let everyone have a few pieces. While you're enjoying this treat, gather together and discuss these questions:

- **Which set of clues was easier to follow and why?** (The first set because it told exactly where to look; the clues were no challenge.)
- **Which set of clues was better, and why?** (The second one, because it lead to the candy.)
- **Do you think it's worth it to look harder and work more to get a reward if you know you've got true clues?**
- **When do we get false clues or lies to follow in life, and what do they lead us to? Think of things that have happened to you or your friends, or things that could easily happen in our family.**

Answer will vary, but could include

• We might be told getting a certain haircut, buying a certain type of clothes, or listening to a certain type of music will make us popular. But these things don't work. We want people to like us for who we really are, not just because we all have the same hairstyle.

• A student or worker might be told that cheating is a sure way to a good grade or getting more money. It's certainly easier than studying or working harder. But the truth is that cheaters only cheat themselves, run the risk of being discovered, and fail the class or lose their job.

• A young person (or even an adult) might feel they need to have sexual relations with a boyfriend or girlfriend in order to feel loved or secure in the relationship. But this lie leads to more insecurity and feelings of guilt and worthlessness.

• We might believe the lie that it's okay to hit, pick on, and otherwise torment our brothers and sisters (after all, isn't that what they're there for?). But the truth is, God made each person in His image and wants us to treat each other with love and respect. Hurting each other leads to unhappiness and poor relationships. Loving others as God wants us to leads to joy and a strong family.

When your family has thought of several examples of how we get mislead by lies, read these verses together and discuss the questions that follow.

Age Adjustments

The discussion might be too long for YOUNG CHILDREN. After they've completed the treasure hunt, read only the Proverbs passage and focus on how children can follow the truth in their lives. For young children this would include obeying parents, telling the truth about who broke the glass (or whatever), and sharing toys even when it's hard.

For OLDER CHILDREN AND TEENAGERS, read and discuss these verses on truth and lies: Isaiah 30:10-11; John 8:32; and John 16:13. What does the Bible teach us about seeking the truth? Why do we replace the truth with lies so often? Why are lies so tempting? How do you see this around you?

ROMANS 1:25

- **Why do people exchange truth for lies?** (Lies seem easier to follow; Satan is always trying to trick us with lies.)
- **What is the result of following lies?** (We get pulled away from God; we start believing things that aren't true.)
- **When do you find it's easier to believe lies? How can you keep your focus on the truth?**

PROVERBS 2:1-5

- **How do we look for truth as if it were a hidden treasure?** (Look for it eagerly, just as we looked for the candy; search until we find it.)
- **Where do we find truth?** (In the Bible; in God.)
- **Why is it worth following the truth even if it's harder than following lies?** (Because the truth always leads to a true treasure; lies are easy to follow but don't have a good reward.)

Share: Sometimes it's hard to follow the truth, especially when others around us want to follow lies. But we know that following lies leads to trouble and disappointment. It's better to work harder and follow the truth because this is God's desire for us and the rewards are everlasting.

WRAP-UP

Gather everyone in a circle and have family members take turns answering this question: **What's one thing you've learned about God today?**

Next, tell kids you've got a new "Life Slogan" you'd like to share with them.

Life Slogan: Today's Life Slogan is this: **"It's best for you to seek what's true!"** Have family members repeat the slogan two or three times to help them learn it. Then encourage them to practice saying it during the week so they can talk about it at your next family night session.

Close in Prayer: Allow time for each family member to share prayer concerns and answers to prayer. Then close your time together with prayer for each concern. Thank God for making families, especially your family! Take time to thank God for each family member, mentioning one special quality you're thankful for about that person.

Remember to record prayer requests here so you can refer to them in the future as you see God answering them.

Additional Resources:

Bible Challenge (ages 6-adult)
Bible Categories (ages 10-adult)
In Other Words game (ages 11-adult)
Smokescreen Secret by Marianne Hering (ages 10+)
Caught in the Act by Janet Holm McHenry (ages 8-10)

☺ 11: The Voice Within

Exploring how our conscience helps us know right from wrong

Scripture
• Romans 2:14-15—God has given a conscience to everyone.
• 1 John 1:9—If we confess our sins, God will forgive us.

ACTIVITY OVERVIEW		
Activity	Summary	Pre-Session Prep
Activity 1: The Nose Knows	Compare how we use our five senses to how we use our consciences.	You'll need strong-smelling foods, a blindfold, and a Bible.
Activity 2: Washed Clean	Discover how to clean our consciences of guilt.	You'll need a piece of dark material, a bowl of bleach, and a Bible.

Main Points:
—Our conscience helps us know right from wrong.
—God can clean our guilty consciences.

LIFE SLOGAN: "I have a conscience that no one can see. The more I listen, the better I'll be."

Make it your own

In the space provided below, outline the flow and add any additional ideas to guide you through the process of conducting this family night.

Prayer & Praise Items

In the space provided below, list any items you wish to pray about or give praise for during this family night session.

Journal

In the space provided below, capture a record of any fun or meaningful things which happened during this family night session.

WARM-UP

Open with Prayer: Begin by having a family member pray, asking God to help everyone in the family understand more about Him through this time. After prayer, review your last lesson by asking these questions:

- **What do you remember from our last lesson?**
- **Do you remember the Life Slogan?**
- **What was one fun thing we did during our last lesson?**
- **How has what we learned last week changed your actions in the past few days?**

Share: Today we'll be learning about what a conscience is and how it helps us know right from wrong.

ACTIVITY 1: The Nose Knows

Point: Our conscience helps us know right from wrong.

Supplies: You'll need a variety of food items with a strong smell (such as an onion, a banana, a lemon, chocolate, and so on), a blindfold, and a Bible. Note: Please be kind to family members and use fresh foods. Don't embarrass anyone by making them sniff at rotting food or anything else disgusting!

Activity: Place the food items under a cloth or in an area where family members cannot see them. Gather your family and ask for a volunteer for an experiment you'd like to conduct.

Blindfold your volunteer, then take one of the food items out from under the cloth and hold it under your child's nose. Ask your child to identify the item you're holding by its smell. When the child guesses correctly, let him or her remove the blindfold, and ask for another child to volunteer. Blindfold this child and choose another food item to be guessed by its smell. Continue until each family member has had a chance to participate. Your kids might even want to blindfold you and run out to the kitchen and choose something for you to sniff!

When everyone has had a turn, put away the food and blindfold, and discuss:

- **What are the five senses?** (Taste, smell, sight, touch, and hearing)
- **Which one did we just use in this experiment?** (Smell)
- **What are ways each of our five senses us help us in life?** Answers will vary, but might include:
  - **Taste:** helps us know if foods are good to eat or bad; helps us enjoy eating.
  - **Smell:** lets us enjoy aromas God has placed around us, such as the scent of flowers; helps us know of smoke nearby; lets us know when dinner's ready!
  - **Sight:** guides us as we move around; lets us see the faces of those we love; lets us read.
  - **Touch:** lets us enjoy being tickled or having our back scratched; helps us know if we're being hurt so we can stop the cause of pain.
  - **Hearing:** lets us enjoy music; helps us communicate; warns us of dangers, such as when a siren blasts or we hear a fire alarm.
- **What happens when one of our senses is damaged and we're unable to use it (like if we become blind or deaf)?** (We have to learn a new way to do things we easily did before; we might not be able to participate in things like we did before, such as not driving if we become blind or not listening to the radio if we become deaf.)

Share: God gave us our five senses to help us enjoy life and help us avoid dangers. God also gave us another sort of sense to help us enjoy life and avoid dangers. It's called our conscience. Do you know what a conscience is?

After family members have given their answers, explain: Our conscience is a part of our mind or soul that reminds us of what is

Age Adjustments

Some CHILDREN might get a better understanding of what conscience is by watching *Pinocchio* on video, or reading a *Pinocchio* storybook. Discuss how Jiminy Cricket serves as Pinocchio's conscience in this story. We don't have a little cricket telling us what's right from wrong, but God tells us. How did Pinocchio learn to listen to Jiminy's voice? How can we learn to listen to God's voice?

For YOUNG CHILDREN, play a game where you tell a simple situation and they tell you whether the actions in the story are right or wrong. For example, "Jessie has a new toy. When her sister wants to look at it, Jessie starts to cry. Is this right or wrong? Why?" Or "Kyle wrote on the wall in his bedroom. Is this right or wrong? Why?" Help children understand that even though we don't always have a Bible verse telling us when to share or when to keep our crayons on the paper, we do have our conscience to help us know right from wrong. Encourage your children by praising them for the times they choose right over wrong.

right and what is wrong. Just like your sight tells you to duck when a baseball is coming toward your head, your conscience tells you that throwing a baseball at your brother's head is wrong! Even people who don't believe in God have a conscience.

Read Romans 2:14-15 together, then **share: This verse tells us that even those who don't know God know in their hearts what is right and wrong. However, people who don't know God don't know what to do with the feelings of guilt they have when they go ahead and do something wrong.**

ACTIVITY 2: Washed Clean

Point: God can clean our guilty consciences.

Supplies: You'll need a small dish of bleach, a dark piece of material, and a Bible.

Share: When we do something wrong, we have a feeling called guilt. What does guilt feel like to you? (Sadness; fear of punishment; a heaviness of heart.)

Bring out the piece of dark material, and **share: When we feel** guilty, it's like our hearts are dirty. Let's imagine our hearts are like this piece of material. It should be white, but it is dark instead.

Place the material in the bleach and set it aside while you continue your discussion.

• **What can you do about guilt?**

After family members have shared what they think can be done about guilt, look to the Bible for an answer.

 Read 1 John 1:9 aloud, then discuss:
• **What does the Bible say we can do about our guilt?** (We can tell God what we've done; we can ask for forgiveness.)
• **Then what does God do?** (He cleans us; He forgives us.)

Remove the material from the bleach. Examine it together to see if it's gotten any whiter. (If not, buy better bleach!)

Share: We can whiten material by soaking it in bleach. We can get our hearts clean of guilt by telling God what we've done, asking for forgiveness, and being washed clean by God. However, if we listen to our conscience in the first place, we won't be sinning and getting into situations where we need to be cleaned!

WRAP-UP

Gather everyone in a circle and have family members take turns answering this question: **What's one thing you've learned about God today?**

Next, tell kids you've got a new "Life Slogan" you'd like to share with them.

Life Slogan: Today's Life Slogan is this: "I have a conscience that no one can see. The more I listen, the better I'll be." Have family members repeat the slogan two or three times to help them learn it. Then encourage them to practice saying it during the week so they can talk about it at your next family night session.

Close in Prayer: Allow time for each family member to share prayer concerns and answers to prayer. Then close your time together with prayer for each concern. Thank God for making families, especially your family! Take time to thank God for each family member, mentioning one special quality you're thankful for about that person.

Remember to record prayer requests here so you can refer to them in the future as you see God answering them.

Additional Resources:

New Teen Choices (ages 12-18)
New Kids Choices (ages 6-12)
Psalms for a Child's Heart by Sheryl Crawford (ages 4-7)

@ 12: It Doesn't Make Sense!

Exploring our need to trust God even when things don't make sense to us

Scripture
• Romans 8:28—God uses even difficult circumstances for His good.
• Job 1–2; and 42—The story of Job.

ACTIVITY OVERVIEW		
Activity	Summary	Pre-Session Prep
Activity 1: I'm Puzzled	Compare challenging puzzles to challenging situations in our lives.	You'll need three different puzzles and a Bible.
Activity 2: The Great Controller	Examine the life of Job to see how God is in control.	You'll need a Bible.

Main Points:

—God can see the plan for our lives even when we can't.

—God cares for us even in hard times.

LIFE SLOGAN: "God the Father knows best!"

Make it your own

In the space provided below, outline the flow and add any additional ideas to guide you through the process of conducting this family night.

Prayer & Praise Items

In the space provided below, list any items you wish to pray about or give praise for during this family night session.

Journal

In the space provided below, capture a record of any fun or meaningful things which happened during this family night session.

WARM-UP

Open with Prayer: Begin by having a family member pray, asking God to help everyone in the family understand more about Him through this time. After prayer, review your last lesson by asking these questions:

- **What do you remember from our last lesson?**
- **Do you remember the Life Slogan?**
- **What was one fun thing we did during our last lesson?**
- **How has what we learned last week changed your actions in the past few days?**

Share: In our time today we'll be learning about how to trust God even when life doesn't make sense to us.

ACTIVITY 1: I'm Puzzled

Point: God can see the plan for our lives even when we can't.

Supplies: You'll need three different 25–50 piece jigsaw puzzles and a Bible.

Activity: Before your time together, set out three different jigsaw puzzles. Place these on different tables, or on the floor in separate locations, so the pieces don't get mixed together. Choose puzzles with a difficulty level appropriate for your children. (Don't use a 1,000-piece puzzle for a four-year-old!) Arrange the puzzles in this way:

Puzzle 1 should be in the correct box.

Puzzle 2 should be in a box, but it should be the wrong box. This means the picture on the box will be different from the actual picture on the puzzle.

Puzzle 3 should have no box or picture of any kind—just pieces.

Bring your family members into the room and have them work on the different puzzles. You can work on each puzzle all together, or break into teams and work on different puzzles at the same time. However, don't make this a competition as this will take away from the focus of the lesson.

When the puzzles have been completed, discuss these questions:

- **What challenge was there to the first puzzle?** (There wasn't much of a challenge; we had the picture to look at, so it wasn't very hard.)
- **What was difficult about the second puzzle?** (We were tricked with the wrong picture! We had to figure out that the picture on the box didn't match the puzzle.)
- **What about the third puzzle? What was tricky about it?** (There was no help at all!)
- **Strange as it seems, these puzzles are like life sometimes. Can you guess why?**

After family members have shared their thoughts, explain: **The first puzzle had a picture that is like a plan for us to follow. In life, God has a plan for us to follow. Sometimes we can see that plan by reading the Bible and we can tell how things should fit together in our lives.**

- **What can we understand about how the pieces of our lives fit together by reading the Bible?** (We can know we're to love each other; the Bible tells us how to treat others; the Bible tells us God should be most important in our lives.)

Share: The second puzzle had the wrong picture. Sometimes we get a picture of how our lives should look in our mind. Maybe we see ourselves with a bigger house, a newer computer, or a faster bike. Just like we first started trying to put together a puzzle we didn't have the pieces for, when we look after this wrong picture of our lives we're working on a life that's not in God's plan. We get led astray by Satan and our own desires, and forget that God knows what the real picture of our lives looks like.

- **Have you ever had a vision for your life, only to discover later that it wasn't right for you?**

Share: The third puzzle had no picture at all. And sometimes in life we simply don't know what's ahead. God knows, because He can tell

what our lives will look like when the pieces are all together, but there are things in our lives God doesn't explain to us.

The Bible says in Romans 8:28 that even the difficult experiences of our lives can be used for God's good purposes. We don't always know what they are, but we can trust that God knows the bigger picture.

Ask if anyone in the family can think of a time when it seemed like they were going through a hard time and didn't understand it all, but it eventually turned out for good. For example, a teacher was very hard to get along with, but through learning about how to do the best in a difficult relationship, the student was later prepared to work with a difficult employer. Or going through a time of little money made you more sympathetic to others in need and helped you become a more generous and giving person. Discuss how difficult it is to be in the middle of a situation where you don't know the outcome, but how we can sometimes look back and see how God used this for good.

ACTIVITY 2: The Great Controller

Point: God cares for us even in hard times.

 Supplies: You'll need a Bible.

Share: The Bible tells us about a man who couldn't understand what was going on in his life. Just like the puzzle with the missing picture, this man was very confused about what God was doing. Let's read about Job.

Read chapters 1–2; and 42 of Job aloud. This is a long story, but interesting to read. If your children are very young, read this story out of a Bible storybook or read the story ahead of time and retell it in your own words. After reading the story, discuss these questions:

- **How would you summarize the story of Job?** (Job is a godly and wealthy man. Then God allows all Job has to be taken away as part of a test. Job and his friends discuss and question why God has allowed this to happen, and finally Job realizes God is in control of life and Job must just be faithful to love and obey God. In the end Job is given more than he had at the beginning.)

- **Why do you think God allowed something bad to happen to Job?** (To show Satan that people don't love God just because of what God provides; to help Job learn that God is in control of the world.)
- **Why do you think bad things happen to good people?** (There is sin in the world; we don't always know why; God allows us to go through tests and difficult times to make us stronger.)

Share: We could just as well ask, why do good things happen to bad people? We learn from Job that we can't know everything about life. We don't see everything the way God does. So even when things are out of control, we can know that God is in control and have trust in Him.

Have one child stand in front of you with his or her back to you. Instruct the child to keep a stiff body and fall backward toward you. Be sure you catch your child! If others want to try this, take turns catching them as well.

 Ask:

- **How is falling in my arms a way of showing you trust me?** (We know you'll catch us and we fall back because we trust you; we know you're big enough to catch us, so we trust you.)
- **Would you trust a person smaller than you to catch you? Why or why not?**

Age Adjustments

YOUNG CHILDREN may still have questions such as "If God is in control, why did my cat Fluffy have to be hit by a car?" Don't stress yourself with trying to come up with a good theological explanation. Admit that we simply don't know. Just as Job didn't know why God had allowed so much suffering in his life, we often don't know why God allows suffering in our lives either. This doesn't mean that God doesn't love us. It just means God can see the bigger picture (like the puzzle) and we can't.

TEENAGERS may feel this discussion is too simplistic. What about evil in the world? Mass murderers? War? Are these things in God's control too? Ask your pastor to discuss the views of your church with you. Look for Christian books that will help teens understand these issues more fully. We know God is in control, but sin is also rampant in our world. How do we fit into this battle and what are our responsibilities?

• **How do we show our trust in God?** (We keep loving God even when we can't see Him holding us up; we love and obey God even when life seems hard.)

Share: It's hard to trust someone small or who has failed us. But God is bigger than us and knows what's best for our lives. We can trust God to catch us and care for us even in hard times.

WRAP-UP

Gather everyone in a circle and have family members take turns answering this question: **What's one thing you've learned about God today?**

Next, tell kids you've got a new "Life Slogan" you'd like to share with them.

Life Slogan: Today's Life Slogan is this: "God the Father knows best!" Have family members repeat the slogan two or three times to help them learn it. Then encourage them to practice saying it during the week so they can talk about it at your next family night session.

Close in Prayer: Allow time for each family member to share prayer concerns and answers to prayer. Then close your time together with prayer for each concern. Thank God for making families, especially your family! Take time to thank God for each family member, mentioning one special quality you're thankful for about that person.

Remember to record prayer requests here so you can refer to them in the future as you see God answering them.

Additional Resources:

He is Risen 55-piece puzzle (ages 7-10)
Noah's Ark puzzle (ages 3-5)
Lightning and Rainbows by Michael Carroll (ages 4-7)
Gold in the Garden by Dorothy Harrison (ages 8-12)
Facing Down the Tough Stuff by Karen Dockrey (ages 8+)

☺ How to Lead Your Child to Christ

SOME THINGS TO CONSIDER AHEAD OF TIME:

1. Realize that God is more concerned about your child's eternal destiny and happiness than you are. "The Lord is not slow in keeping his promise. . . . He is patient with you, not wanting anyone to perish, but everyone to come to repentance" (2 Peter 3:9).

2. Pray specifically beforehand that God will give you insights and wisdom in dealing with each child on his or her maturity level.

3. Don't use terms like "take Jesus into your heart," "dying and going to hell," and "accepting Christ as your personal Savior." Children are either too literal ("How does Jesus breathe in my heart?") or the words are too clichéd and trite for their understanding.

4. Deal with each child alone, and don't be in a hurry. Make sure he or she understands. Discuss. Take your time.

A FEW CAUTIONS:

1. When drawing children to Himself, Jesus said for others to "allow" them to come to Him (see Mark 10:14). Only with adults did He use the term "compel" (see Luke 14:23). Do not compel children.

2. Remember that unless the Holy Spirit is speaking to the child, there will be no genuine heart experience of regeneration. Parents, don't get caught up in the idea that Jesus will return the day before you were going to speak to your child about salvation and that it will be too late. Look at God's character— He *is* love! He is not dangling your child's soul over hell. Wait on God's timing.

Pray with faith, believing. Be concerned, but don't push.

THE PLAN:

1. **God loves you.** Recite John 3:16 with your child's name in place of "the world."

2. **Show the child his or her need of a Savior.**

   a. Deal with sin carefully. There is one thing that cannot enter heaven—sin.

   b. Be sure your child knows what sin is. Ask him to name some (things common to children—lying, sassing, disobeying, etc.). Sin is doing or thinking anything wrong according to God's Word. It is breaking God's Law.

   c. Ask the question "Have you sinned?" If the answer is no, do not continue. Urge him to come and talk to you again when he does feel that he has sinned. Dismiss him. You may want to have prayer first, however, thanking God "for this young child who is willing to do what is right." Make it easy for him to talk to you again, but do not continue. Do not say, "Oh, yes, you have too sinned!" and then name some. With children, wait for God's conviction.

   d. If the answer is yes, continue. He may even give a personal illustration of some sin he has done recently or one that has bothered him.

   e. Tell him what God says about sin: We've all sinned ("There is no one righteous, not even one," Rom. 3:10). And because of that sin, we can't get to God ("For the wages of sin is death . . . " Rom. 6:23). So He had to come to us (". . . but the gift of God is eternal life in Christ Jesus our Lord," Rom. 6:23).

   f. Relate God's gift of salvation to Christmas gifts—we don't earn them or pay for them; we just accept them and are thankful for them.

3. **Bring the child to a definite decision.**

   a. Christ must be received if salvation is to be possessed.

   b. Remember, do not force a decision.

   c. Ask the child to pray out loud in her own words. Give her some things she could say if she seems unsure. Now be prepared for a blessing! (It is best to avoid having the child repeat a memorized prayer after you. Let her think, and make it personal.)*

d. After salvation has occurred, pray for her out loud. This is a good way to pronounce a blessing on her.

4. **Lead your child into assurance.**

Show him that he will have to keep his relationship open with God through repentance and forgiveness (just like with his family or friends), but that God will always love him ("Never will I leave you; never will I forsake you," Heb. 13:5).

* If you wish to guide your child through the prayer, here is some suggested language.

> *"Dear God, I know that I am a sinner [have child name specific sins he or she acknowledged earlier, such as lying, stealing, disobeying, etc.]. I know that Jesus died on the cross to pay for all my sins. I ask You to forgive me of my sins. I believe that Jesus died for me and rose from the dead, and I accept Him as my Savior. Thank You for loving me. In Jesus' name. Amen."*

Cumulative Topical Index

TOPIC	SCRIPTURE	WHAT YOU'LL NEED	WHERE TO FIND IT
The Acts of the Sinful Nature and the Fruit of the Spirit	Gal. 5:19-26	3x5 cards or paper, markers, and tape	IFN, p. 43
All Have Sinned	Rom. 3:23	Raw eggs, bucket of water	BCB, p. 89
Avoid Things that keep us from growing	Eph. 4:14-15; Heb. 5:11-14	Seeds, plants at various stages of growth or a garden or nursery to tour, Bible	CCQ, p. 77
Bad Company Corrupts Good Character	1 Cor. 15:33	Small ball, string, slips of paper, pencil, yarn or masking tape, Bible	IFN, p. 103
Be Thankful for Good Friends		Bible, art supplies, markers	IFN, p. 98
Being Content with What We Have	Phil. 4:11-13	Bible	CCQ, p. 17
Change Helps Us Grow and Mature	Rom. 8:28-39	Bible	WLS, p. 39
Christ Is Who We Serve	Col. 3:23-24	Paper, scissors, pens	IFN, p. 50
Christians should be joyful each day	James 3:22-23; Ps. 118:24	Small plastic bottle, cork to fit bottle opening, water, vinegar, paper towel, Bible	CCQ, p. 67
Commitment and hard work are needed to finish strong	Gen. 6:5-22	Jigsaw puzzle, Bible	CCQ, p. 83
The Consequence of Sin Is Death	Ps. 19:1-6	Dominoes	BCB, p. 57
Creation	Gen. 1:1; Ps. 19:1-6; Rom. 1:20	Nature book or video, Bible	IFN, p. 17
David and Bathsheba	2 Sam. 11:1–12:14	Bible	BCB, p. 90
Description of Heaven	Rev. 21:3-4, 10-27	Bible, drawing supplies	BCB, p. 76
Difficulty can Help Us Grow	Jer. 32:17; Luke 18:27	Bible, card game like Old Maid or Crazy Eight	CCQ, p. 33

AN
INTRODUCTION
TO FAMILY
NIGHTS
= IFN

BASIC
CHRISTIAN
BELIEFS
= BCB

CHRISTIAN
CHARACTER
QUALITIES
= CCQ

WISDOM LIFE
SKILLS
= WLS

TOPIC	SCRIPTURE	WHAT YOU'LL NEED	WHERE TO FIND IT
Discipline and Training Make Us Stronger	Prov. 4:23	Narrow doorway, Bible	CCQ, p. 103
Don't Be Yoked with Unbelievers	2 Cor. 16:17–17:1	Milk, food coloring	IFN, p. 105
Don't Give Respect Based on Material Wealth	Eph. 6:1-8; 1 Peter 2:13-17; Ps. 119:17; James 2:1-2; 1 Tim. 4:12	Large sheet of paper, tape, a pen, Bible	IFN, p. 64
Equality Does Not Mean Contentment	Matt. 20:1-16	Money or candy bars, tape recorder or radio, Bible	WLS, p. 21
Even if We're not in the Majority, We May be Right	2 Tim. 3:12-17	Piece of paper, pencil, water	CCQ, p. 95
Every Day Is a Gift From God	Prov. 16:9	Bible	CCQ, p. 69
Evil Hearts Say Evil Words	Prov. 15:2-8; Luke 6:45; Eph. 4:29	Bible, small mirror	IFN, p. 79
The Fruit of the Spirit	Gal. 5:22-23; Luke 3:8; Acts 26:20	Blindfold and Bible	BCB, p. 92
God Allows Testing to Help Us Mature	James 1:2-4	Bible	BCB, p. 44
God Can Clean Our Guilty Consciences	1 John 1:9	Small dish of bleach, dark piece of material, Bible	WLS, p. 95
God Can Do the Impossible	John 6:1-14	Bible, sturdy plank (6 or more inches wide and 6 to 8 feet long), a brick or similar object, snack of fish and crackers	CCQ, p. 31
God Can Guide Us Away from Satan's Traps	Ps. 119:9-11; Prov. 3:5-6	Ten or more inexpensive mousetraps, pencil, blindfold, Bible	WLS, p. 72
God Can Help Us Knock Sin Out of Our Lives	Ps. 32:1-5; 1 John 1:9	Heavy drinking glass, pie tin, small slips of paper, pencils, large raw egg, cardboard tube from a roll of toilet paper, broom, masking tape, Bible	WLS, p. 53
God Cares for Us Even in Hard Times	Job 1–2; 42	Bible	WLS, p. 103
God Created Us	Isa. 45:9, 64:8; Ps. 139:13	Bible and video of potter with clay	BCB, p. 43
God Doesn't Want Us to Worry	Matt. 6:25-34; Phil. 4:6-7; Ps.55:22	Bible, paper, pencils	CCQ, p. 39

TOPIC	SCRIPTURE	WHAT YOU'LL NEED	WHERE TO FIND IT
God Forgives Those Who Confess Their Sins	1 John 1:9	Sheets of paper, tape, Bible	BCB, p. 58
God Gave Jesus a Message for Us	John 1:14,18; 8:19; 12:49-50	Goldfish in water or bug in jar, water	BCB, p. 66
God Gives and God Can Take Away	Luke 12:13-21	Bible, timer with bell or buzzer, large bowl of small candies, smaller bowl for each child	CCQ, p. 15
God Is Holy	Ex. 3:1-6	Masking tape, baby powder or corn starch, broom, Bible	IFN, p. 31
God Is Invisible, Powerful, and Real	John 1:18, 4:24; Luke 24:36-39	Balloons, balls, refrigerator magnets, Bible	IFN, p. 15
God Knew His Plans for Us	Jer. 29:11	Two puzzles and a Bible	BCB, p. 19
God Knows All About Us	Ps. 139:2-4; Matt. 10:30	3x5 cards, a pen	BCB, p. 17
God Knows Everything	Isa. 40:13-14; Eph. 4:1-6	Bible	IFN, p. 15
God Knows the Plan for Our Lives	Rom. 8:28	Three different 25–50 piece jigsaw puzzles, Bible	WLS, p. 101
God Loves Us So Much, He Sent Jesus	John 3:16; Eph. 2:8-9	I.O.U. for each family member	IFN, p. 34
God Made Our Family Unique by Placing Each of Us in It		Different color paint for each family member, toothpicks or paintbrushes to dip into paint, white paper, Bible	BCB, p. 110
God Made Us in His Image	Gen. 1:24-27	Play dough or clay and Bible	BCB, p. 24
God Never Changes	Ecc. 3:1-8; Heb. 13:8	Paper, pencils, Bible	WLS, p. 37
God Provides a Way Out of Temptation	1 Cor. 10:12-13; James 1:13-14; 4:7; 1 John 2:15-17	Bible	IFN, p. 88
God Wants Us to be Diligent in Our Work	Prov. 6:6-11; 1 Thes. 4:11-12	Video about ants or picture books or encyclopedia; Bible	CCQ, p. 55
God Wants Us to Get Closer to Him	James 4:8; 1 John 4:7-12	Hidden Bibles, clues to find them	BCB, p. 33
God Wants Us to Glorify Him	Ps. 24:1; Luke 12:13-21	Paper, pencils, Bible	WLS, p. 47
God Wants Us to Work and Be Helpful	2 Thes. 3:6-15	Several undone chores, Bible	CCQ, p. 53

Family Night
TOOL CHEST

AN INTRODUCTION TO FAMILY NIGHTS
= IFN

BASIC CHRISTIAN BELIEFS
= BCB

CHRISTIAN CHARACTER QUALITIES
= CCQ

WISDOM LIFE SKILLS
= WLS

AN
INTRODUCTION
TO FAMILY
NIGHTS
= IFN

BASIC
CHRISTIAN
BELIEFS
= BCB

CHRISTIAN
CHARACTER
QUALITIES
= CCQ

WISDOM LIFE
SKILLS
= WLS

TOPIC	SCRIPTURE	WHAT YOU'LL NEED	WHERE TO FIND IT
God Will Send the Holy Spirit	John 14:23-26; 1 Cor. 2:12	Flashlights, small treats, Bible	IFN, p. 39
God's Covenant with Noah	Gen. 8:13-21; 9:8-17	Bible, paper, crayons or markers	BCB, p. 52
Guarding the Gate to Our Minds	Prov. 4:13; 2 Cor. 11:3; Phil. 4:8	Bible, poster board for each family member, old magazines, glue, scissors, markers	CCQ, p. 23
The Holy Spirit Helps Us	Eph. 1:17; John 14:15-17; Acts 1:1-11; Eph. 3:16-17; Rom. 8:26-27; 1 Cor. 2:11-16	Bible	BCB, p. 99
Honor the Holy Spirit, Don't Block Him	1 John 4:4; 1 Cor. 6:19-20	Bible, blow dryer or vacuum cleaner with exit hose, a ping pong ball	CCQ, p. 47
Honor Your Parents	Ex. 20:12	Paper, pencil, treats, umbrella, soft objects, masking tape, pen, Bible	IFN, p. 55
It's Better to Follow the Truth	Rom. 1:25; Prov. 2:1-5	Second set of clues, box of candy or treats, Bible	WLS, p. 86
It's Easy to Follow a Lie, but It Leads to Disappointment		Clues as described in lesson, empty box	WLS, p. 85
The Importance of Your Name Being Written in the Book of Life	Rev. 20:11-15; 21:27	Bible, phone book, access to other books with family name	BCB, p. 74
It's Important to Listen to Jesus' Message		Bible	BCB, p. 68
Jesus Dies on the Cross	John 14:6	6-foot 2x4, 3-foot 2x4, hammers, nails, Bible	IFN, p. 33
Jesus Took the Punishment We Deserve	Rom. 6:23; John 3:16; Rom. 5:8-9	Bathrobe, list of bad deeds	IFN, p. 26
Jesus Washes His Followers' Feet	John 13:1-17	Bucket of warm, soapy water, towels, Bible	IFN, p. 63
Joshua and the Battle of Jericho	Josh. 1:16-18; 6:1-21	Paper, pencil, dots on paper that when connected form a star	IFN, p. 57

TOPIC	SCRIPTURE	WHAT YOU'LL NEED	WHERE TO FIND IT
Knowing God's Word Helps Us Know What Stand to Take	2 Tim. 3:1-5	Current newspaper, Bible	CCQ, p. 93
Look to God, Not Others	Phil. 4:11-13	Magazines or newspapers, a chair, several pads of small yellow stickies, Bible	WLS, p. 24
Loving Money Is Wrong	1 Tim. 6:6-10	Several rolls of coins, masking tape, Bible	WLS, p. 45
The More We Know God, the More We Know His Voice	John 10:1-6	Bible	BCB, p. 35
Nicodemus Asks Jesus About Being Born Again	John 3:7, 50-51; 19:39-40	Bible, paper, pencil, costume	BCB, p. 81
Obedience Has Good Rewards		Planned outing everyone will enjoy, directions on 3x5 cards, number cards	IFN, p. 59
Only a Relationship with God Can Fill Our Need	Isa. 55:1-2	Doll that requires batteries, batteries for the doll, dollar bill, pictures of a house, an expensive car, and a pretty woman or handsome man, Bible	WLS, p. 62
Our Conscience Helps Us Know Right from Wrong	Rom. 2:14-15	Foods with a strong smell, blindfold, Bible	WLS, p. 93
Our Minds Should Be Filled with Good, Not Evil	Phil 4:8; Ps. 119:9, 11	Bible, bucket of water, several large rocks	CCQ, p. 26
Parable of the Talents	Matt. 25:14-30	Bible	IFN, p. 73
Parable of the Vine and Branches	John 15:1-8	Tree branch, paper, pencils, Bible	IFN, p. 95
Persecution Brings a Reward		Bucket, bag of ice, marker, one-dollar bill	WLS, p. 32
Planning Helps Us Finish Strong	Phil. 3:10-14	Flight map on p. 86, paper, pencils, Bible	CCQ, p. 85
Pray, Endure, and Be Glad When We're Persecuted	Matt. 5:11-12, 44; Rom. 12:14; 1 Cor. 4:12	Notes, Bible, candle or flashlight, dark small space	WLS, p. 29
The Responsibiities of Families	Eph. 5:22-33; 6:1-4	Photo albums, Bible	BCB, p. 101
Satan Looks for Ways to Trap Us	Luke 4:1-13	Cardboard box, string, stick, small ball, Bible	WLS, p. 69

AN INTRODUCTION TO FAMILY NIGHTS
= IFN

BASIC CHRISTIAN BELIEFS
= BCB

CHRISTIAN CHARACTER QUALITIES
= CCQ

WISDOM LIFE SKILLS
= WLS

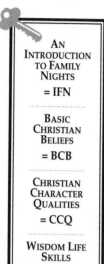

AN
INTRODUCTION
TO FAMILY
NIGHTS
= IFN

BASIC
CHRISTIAN
BELIEFS
= BCB

CHRISTIAN
CHARACTER
QUALITIES
= CCQ

WISDOM LIFE
SKILLS
= WLS

TOPIC	SCRIPTURE	WHAT YOU'LL NEED	WHERE TO FIND IT
Self-control Helps Us Resist the Enemy	1 Peter 5:8-9; 1 Peter 2:11-12	Blindfold, watch or timer, feather or other "tickly" item, Bible	CCQ, p. 101
Serve One Another in Love	Gal. 5:13	Bag of small candies, at least three per child	IFN, p. 47
Sin and Busyness Interfere with Our Prayers	Luke 10:38-42; Ps. 46:10; Matt. 5:23-24; 1 Peter 3:7	Bible, two paper cups, two paper clips, long length of fishing line	CCQ, p. 61
Sin Separates Humanity	Gen. 3:1-24	Bible, clay creations, piece of hardened clay or play dough	BCB, p. 25
Some Places Aren't Open to Everyone		Book or magazine with "knock-knock" jokes	BCB, p. 73
Some Things in Life Are Out of Our Control		Blindfolds	BCB, p. 41
Temptation Takes Our Eyes Off God		Fishing pole, items to catch, timer, Bible	IFN, p. 85
Those Who Don't Believe Are Foolish	Ps. 44:1	Ten small pieces of paper, pencil, Bible	IFN, p. 19
The Tongue Is Small but Powerful	James 3:3-12	Video, news magazine or picture book showing devastation of fire, match, candle, Bible	IFN, p. 77
Trials Help Us Grow	James 1:2-4	Sugar cookie dough, cookie cutters, baking sheets, miscellaneous baking supplies, Bible	WLS, p. 15
Trials Test How We've Grown	James 1:12	Bible	WLS, p. 17
We All Sin	Rom. 3:23	Target and items to throw	IFN, p. 23
We Can Communicate with Each Other			BCB, p. 65
We Can Help Each Other	Prov. 27:17	Masking tape, bowl of unwrapped candies, rulers, yardsticks, or dowel rods	BCB, p. 110
We Can Love by Helping Those in Need	Heb. 13:1-3		IFN, p. 48
We Can Show Love Through Respecting Family Members		Paper and pen	IFN, p. 66

TOPIC	SCRIPTURE	WHAT YOU'LL NEED	WHERE TO FIND IT
We Can't Take Back the Damage of Our Words		Tube of toothpaste for each child, $10 bill	IFN, p. 78
We Deserve Punishment for Our Sins	Rom. 6:23	Dessert, other materials as decided	IFN, p. 24
We Have All We Need in Our Lives	Ecc. 3:11	Paper, pencils, Bible	WLS, p. 61
We Have a New Life in Christ	John 3:3; 2 Cor. 5:17	Video or picture book of caterpillar forming a cocoon then a butterfly, or a tadpole becoming a frog, or a seed becoming a plant	BCB, p. 93
We Know Others by Our Relationships with Them		Copies of questionnaire, pencils, Bible	BCB, p. 31
We Must Be in Constant Contact with God		Blindfold	CCQ, p. 63
We Must Choose to Obey		3x5 cards or slips of paper, markers, and tape	IFN, p. 43
We Must Either Choose Christ or Reject Christ	Matt. 12:30	Clear glass jar, cooking oil, water, spoon, Bible	CCQ, p. 96
We Must Learn How Much Responsibility We Can Handle		Building blocks, watch with second hand, paper, pencil	IFN, p. 71
We Must Listen	Prov. 1:5, 8-9; 4:1	Bible, other supplies for the task you choose	WLS, p. 77
We Must Think Before We Speak	James 1:19	Bible	WLS, p. 79
We Need to Grow Physically, Emotionally, and Spiritually	1 Peter 2:2	Photograph albums or videos of your children at different ages, tape measure, bathroom scale, Bible	CCQ, p. 75
We Reap What We Sow	Gal. 6:7	Candy bar, Bible	IFN, p. 55
We Shouldn't Value Possessions Over Everything Else	1 Tim. 6:7-8	Box is optional	CCQ, p. 18
With Help, Life Is a Lot Easier		Supplies to do the chore you choose	BCB, p. 101
Wolves in Sheeps' Clothing	Matt. 7:15-20	Ten paper sacks, a marker, ten small items, Bible	IFN, p. 97

Family Night
TOOL CHEST

AN INTRODUCTION TO FAMILY NIGHTS
= IFN

BASIC CHRISTIAN BELIEFS
= BCB

CHRISTIAN CHARACTER QUALITIES
= CCQ

WISDOM LIFE SKILLS
= WLS

AN
INTRODUCTION
TO FAMILY
NIGHTS
= IFN

BASIC
CHRISTIAN
BELIEFS
= BCB

CHRISTIAN
CHARACTER
QUALITIES
= CCQ

WISDOM LIFE
SKILLS
= WLS

TOPIC	SCRIPTURE	WHAT YOU'LL NEED	WHERE TO FIND IT
Worrying Doesn't Change Anything		Board, inexpensive doorbell buzzer, a 9-volt battery, extra length of electrical wire, a large belt, assorted tools	CCQ, p. 37
You Look Like the Person in Whose Image You Are Created		Paper roll, crayons, markers, pictures of your kids and of yourself as a child	BCB, p. 23

About
Heritage Builders

OUR VISION

To build a network of families, churches, and individuals committed to passing a strong family heritage to the next generation and to support one another in that effort.

OUR VALUES

Family—We believe that the traditional, intact family provides the most stable and healthy environment for passing a strong heritage to the next generation, but that non-intact homes can also successfully pass a solid heritage.

Faith—We believe that many of the principles for passing a solid heritage are effective regardless of one's religious tradition, but that the Christian faith provides the only lasting foundation upon which to build a strong family heritage.

Values—We believe that there are certain moral absolutes which govern our world and serve as the foundation upon which a strong heritage should be built, and that the current trend toward value neutrality is unraveling the heritage fabric of future generations.

Church—We believe that all families need a support network and that the local church is the institution of choice for helping families successfully pass a strong heritage to the next generation.

OUR BELIEFS

We embrace the essential tenets of orthodox Christianity as summarized by the National Association of Evangelicals:

1. *We believe the Bible to be the inspired, the only infallible, authoritative Word of God.*

2. *We believe that there is one God, eternally existent in three persons: Father, Son, and Holy Ghost.*

3. *We believe in the deity of our Lord Jesus Christ, in His virgin birth, in His sinless life, in His miracles, in His vicarious and atoning death through His shed blood, in His bodily resurrection, in His ascension to the right hand of the Father, and in His personal return in power and glory.*

4. *We believe that for the salvation of lost and sinful people, regeneration by the Holy Spirit is absolutely essential.*

5. *We believe in the present ministry of the Holy Spirit, by whose indwelling the Christian is enabled to live a godly life.*

6. *We believe in the resurrection of both the saved and the lost; they that are saved unto the resurrection of life and they that are lost unto the resurrection of damnation.*

7. *We believe in the spiritual unity of believers in our Lord Jesus Christ.*

OUR PEOPLE

Heritage Builders is lead by a team of family life experts.

Cofounder - J. Otis Ledbetter, Ph.D.
Married over 25 years to Gail, two grown children, one teenager
Pastor, Chestnut Baptist Church in Clovis, California
Author - *The Heritage, Family Fragrance*

Cofounder - Kurt Bruner, M.A.
Married over 12 years to Olivia, three young sons
Vice President, Focus on the Family Resource Group
Author - *The Heritage, Family Night Tool Chest* Series

Cofounder - Jim Weidmann
Married over 15 years to Janet, two sons, two daughters
Family Night Training Consultant
Author - *Family Night Tool Chest* Series

Senior Associates - Heritage Builders draws upon the collective wisdom of various authors, teachers, and parents who provide resources, motivation, and advice for the heritage passing process.

BECOME A HERITAGE BUILDER IN YOUR COMMUNITY!

We seek to fulfill our mission by sponsoring the following.

HERITAGE BUILDERS RESOURCES - Products specifically designed to motivate and assist parents in the heritage passing process.

HERITAGE WORKSHOP - Using various formats, this seminar teaches attendees the principles and tools for passing a solid heritage, and helps them create a highly practical action plan for doing so.

HERITAGE BUILDERS NETWORK - A network of churches which have established an ongoing heritage builder support ministry where families can help families through mutual encouragement and creativity.

HERITAGE BUILDERS NEWSLETTER - We provide a forum through which families can share heritage building success stories and tips in our periodic newsletter.

If you are interested in hosting a Heritage Workshop, launching a Heritage Builders ministry in your local church, learning about new Heritage Building resources, receiving our newsletter, or becoming a Heritage Builder Associate, contact us by writing, phoning, or visiting our web site.

Heritage Builders Association
c/o ChariotVictor Publishing
4050 Lee Vance View
Colorado Springs, CO 80918
or call: 1-800-528-9489 (7 A.M.– 4:30 P.M. MST)
www.chariotvictor.com
or
www.heritagebuilders.com

HERITAGE BUILDERS

☐ Please send me a FREE One-Year Subscription to Heritage Builders Newsletter.

Name _____

Address _____

City _____ State ____ Zip _____ Phone _____

Church Affiliation _____

E-mail Address _____

Signature _____